Lecture Notes in Computer Science

Lecture Notes in Computer Science

Edited by G. Goos and J. Hartmanis

77

Gregor v. Bochmann

Architecture of Distributed Computer Systems

Springer-Verlag
Berlin Heidelberg New York 1979

Gregor v. Bochmann
Université de Montréal
Dépt. d'Informatique et de
Recherche Opérationelle (I.R.O.)
Case Postale 6128
Succursale "1"
Montréal, P.R.H3C 3J7
Canada

AMS Subject Classifications (1970): 68 A 05, 68 B 20, 94 A xx
CR Subject Classifications (1974): 3.8, 4.3, 6.0

ISBN 3-540-09723-6 Springer-Verlag Berlin Heidelberg New York
ISBN 0-387-09723-6 Springer-Verlag New York Heidelberg Berlin

Library of Congress Cataloging in Publication Data
Bochmann, Gregor v. 1941-
Architecture of distributed computer systems.
(Lecture notes in computer science; 77)
Bibliography: p.
Includes index.
1. Electronic data processing--Distributed processing. 2. Computer architecture.
I. Title. II. Series.
QA76.9.D5B63 001.6'4 79-24491
ISBN 0-387-09723-6

© by Springer-Verlag Berlin Heidelberg 1979
Printed in Germany

Printing and binding: Beltz Offsetdruck, Hemsbach/Bergstr.
2145/3140-543210

P R E F A C E

This text is written for computer programmers, analysts and scientists, as well as computer science students, as an introduction to the architecture of distributed computer systems. The emphasis is placed on a clear understanding of the principles, rather than on details; and the reader will learn about the structure of distributed systems, their problems, and approaches to their design and development. The reader should have a basic knowledge of computer systems and be familiar with modular design principles for software development. He should also be aware of present-day remote-access and distributed computer applications.

The first part of the text serves as an introduction to the concept of "distributed system". We give examples, try to define terms, and discuss the problems that arise in the context of parallel and distributed processing. The second part deals with the description of parallelism, making abstraction from the physical distribution of the different system components. We discuss formalized methods that may be used to specify, and analyse the behaviour of, parallelism in local operating systems or distributed computer systems. In the third part, we explain the architecture of distributed systems and the role of the different communication protocols used. This includes the discussion of data transmission networks, as well as so-called higher level protocols used in computer networks for communication between different application programs, data bases, and terminals.

This text does not give the description of any particular distributed system, nor does it discuss the advantages and disadvantages of distributed computer applications, such as for banking transactions or distributed data bases. We have given extensive references to more detailed descriptions of the topics discussed, to complementary articles, and to explanations of certain prerequisite concepts, most readers will be familiar with.

This text was written when the author was a visiting

professor at the Ecole Polytechnique Fédérale de Lausanne,
Switzerland. It represents the lecture notes of a one-semester
course ("troisième cycle") given in the Département de Mathématiques in 1977-78. I would like to thank the Département de
Mathématiques, and in particular Professor G. Coray, for my
pleasant stay in Lausanne. For the preparation of this text,
I have profited from many discussions, in particular with
J. Gecsei (Montreal), D. Gurtner and F. Vittoz. I thank
S. Waddell for suggesting many improvements of the original
manuscript, and Ch. Luyet and D. Salconi (Montreal) for the
careful typing. Last, but not least, I thank my wife, Elise,
for her patience and moral support.

TABLE OF CONTENTS

CHAPTER I

DISTRIBUTED SYSTEMS : DEFINITION AND EXAMPLES

What is a distributed system ? - Most data processing systems are of a distributed nature, and most computer systems can be considered as being distributed under certain aspects. This chapter presents some common examples of data processing and computing systems and discusses in particular the aspects of parallelism and distribution of control and data. Some classification schemes are explained, and a definition of "distributed systems" is attempted.

1.1. *DISTRIBUTION OF CONTROL AND DATA IN EXISTING SYSTEMS*

The following examples of existing systems demonstrate how control information and data may be distributed over the different components of a data processing system, which may imply distributed processing and decisions, as well as distributed algorithms.

1.1.1. *Systems distributed over long distance*

1.1.1.1. Remote access

With the advent of multi-programming systems, which provide data processing services to several applications simultaneously, it became desirable to obtain access to such facilities from terminals at different locations. It has become common practice to exchange data between terminals and computer systems through telephone circuits, as shown in figure 1.1, using modems for the adaptation of the digital interfaces of the terminals and computer systems to the analogue nature of the telephone transmission facility. Leased circuits, providing a dedicated connection between two or more system components, are often used as an economic alternative to frequent connections established through the public

2

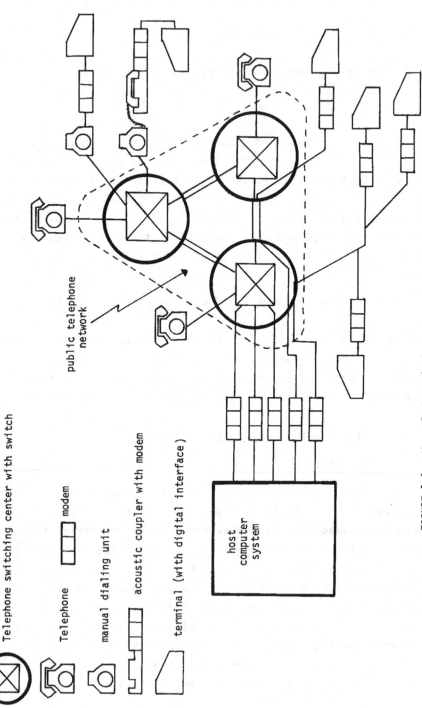

Telephone switching center with switch

Telephone

manual dialing unit

modem

acoustic coupler with modem

terminal (with digital interface)

public telephone network

host computer system

FIGURE 1.1: Use of the telephone network for data transmission

3

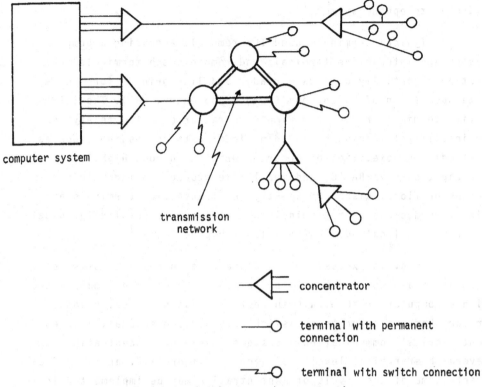

FIGURE 1.2: Multiplexing and concentration

switched telephone system.[1]

Typical terminals used for remotely accessing a computer system are interactive terminals and remote batch terminals, consisting essentially of a card reader and line printer for the remote submission of batch jobs (remote job entry, RJE). The interactive terminals range from simple character oriented teletypes to intelligent terminals providing local data processing, such as text editing, execution of programs written in some high-level language, such as BASIC, and local file storage on magnetic cassettes or floppy disks. Data entry and transaction terminals are widely used classes of terminals of intermediate complexity, usually providing local editing on a line or page basis.[2]

To avoid excessive long distance transmission costs, concentrators are used when several terminals in one area communicate with a computer or terminals in another, distant, area. A concentrator shares a given transmission path between several, independent, logical communications. Systems involving concentration at several hierarchical levels, as shown in figure 1.2, are very frequent. Some of the levels of concentration may be implemented inside the transmission network without the knowledge of the subscriber For example, the wide band trunk lines between the telephone switching centers are shared among a large number of simultaneous long distance switched telephone connections and leased telephone circuits. Similar configurations are used with the new public data networks providing permanent (leased) or switched (possibly virtual) circuits, based on digital transmission technology with lower error rates.[3]

Two different kinds of concentration may be distinguished for data transmission.[4] The simplest method is known as "multiplexing" (frequency division multiplexing for analogue transmissions, such as telephony, and time division multiplexing for digital transmission). In this case, the available transmission capacity of the shared channel is divided in a fixed ratio among a certain number of secondary channels.

A more flexible method is known as "statistical multiplexing" or "concentration". In this case, the available capacity is allocated to the different channels in a varying ratio depending on the demand. Data is transmitted in the form of blocks (packets or messages) each containing same control information, which is used in particular to identify the secondary channel to which the data belongs. Because of the varying transmission demands of the different secondary channels, data blocks may be put on a queue, to await transmission at the earliest possibility. Depending on the amount of data traffic and the capacity of the shared channel, this queuing introduces an additional, statistically varying transmission delay.[5]

Statistical multiplexing is usually implemented on minicomputer systems. Often these systems also provide for the adaptation of the terminals, which are connected on to the secondary channels, to the data transmission facility and the communication protocols of the distant host computer system. This function is called "terminal handling", and consists mainly of the assembly (and disassembly) of characters exchanged with the terminal into (from) data blocks exchanged over the shared channel with the distant host.

The host computer system is closely related to the design of the remote access communication system. In many cases, the communication system was built around existing host computer systems, and the latter had a strong impact on the design of the former. In particular, the following parts of the host operating system have a counterpart in the distributed communication system :

- The handling of interactive terminals in the operating system and the remote concentrators is related.

- The handling of files by the operating system and the operation of remote job entry stations is related.

- The concentration protocol used over the shared access lines must be implemented in the concentrators and the operating system of the host.

Often, in order to reserve the processing power of the host computer for the application program, many of the communication functions of the operating system are realized in a specialized front-end mini-computer.

Some well-known applications of remote access systems as described above are :

- passenger reservation systems for air travel,
- banking systems,
- sale and inventory systems for warehouses and super-markets,
- computer applications service companies, etc.

1.1.1.2. Computer networks

While the systems discussed above provide access to a single host computer, computer networks provide access from terminals to several host computers, and also communication between application programs residing in different computers. The main reasons for the construction of computer networks are[6]

(1) to provide remote access to a variety of resources, for example normal data processing, special facilities such as high power numerical calculations, graphical applications, etc., access to data bases, a facility for exchanging personal messages, etc.;

(2) to share these resources among a large number of users;

(3) to provide back-up facilities in the case of the failure of one of the resources;

(4) to provide a reliable communication medium for the remote accessing of resources and for distributed processing involving several resources.

The experimental networks Arpanet[7] (in the US) and Cyclades[8] (in France) were developed in the late sixties and early seventies to gain experience with computer networks. The architecture of these networks is shown in figure 1.3. The data transmission. sub-network is responsible for the exchange of data between the connected computers and terminals. An irregular topology with multiple paths between any two network nodes provides for reliable service, even in the case of occasional failures of transmission circuits and intermediate nodes.

The concept of "packet switching" is used in these networks, which means that the data exchanged among the computers and terminals is transmitted through the sub-network in the form of data packets with a typical length of about one line of text or up to some thousand bits. The individual packets are transmitted through the sub-network more or less independently of each other, depending on the design of the network.

The sharing of transmission circuits between different applications is realized at several levels. The access circuit between a computer and the sub-network is usually shared among a large number of communications involving this computer and several terminals and other computers. The high-speed transmission circuits between the nodes of the sub-network are shared between the data traffic of all users and some control traffic of the sub-network. Since statistical multiplexing is used, the end-to-end transmission delay for data packets varies and is usually of the order of several hundred milliseconds, sufficiently short for interactive applications, but noticeably longer than the delay over dedicated or switched circuits.

After the pioneering work of Arpanet and Cyclades, many private computer networks have been built using similar approaches. Also, some of the communications software packages provided by computer manufacturers for their systems provide similar functions. Most of these systems and networks use as their

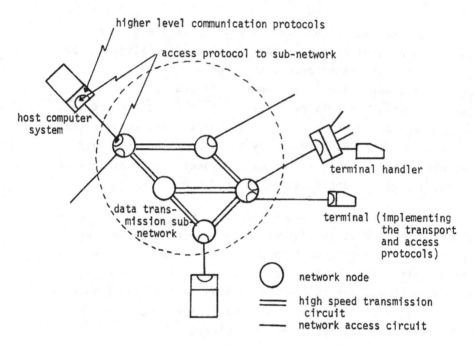

FIGURE 1.3: Typical architecture of a computer network.

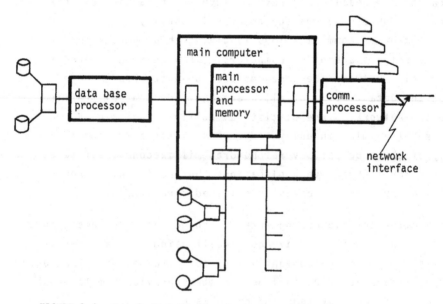

FIGURE 1.4: Local distribution in a computer system

transmission facility the public service of leased circuits provided by common carriers. It is only recently that some common
carriers have introduced public data transmission facilities based on packet switching[9]. Public packet-switched data networks,
similar to the data transmission sub-networks of Arpanet and
Cyclades, can be used for remote access to host computers and
computer-computer communications.

An important aspect of the Arpanet and Cyclades computer
networks is the "heterogenity" of the connected host computers and
their operating systems. Realizing meaningful communications between application programs, terminals, files and data bases on
different computers requires some agreement on so-called higher
level protocols. These protocols, implemented in the communication software of the connected computers and terminals, provide
end-to-end data transport between the communicating entities,
and access to terminals, files, etc.. It is clearly very important to develop protocol standards which are suitable for future
systems and allow for easy adaptation of the conventions used in
present operating systems.[10]

In the absence of such standards, it is difficult to
implement communications between heterogeneous computer systems,
either within a computer network or directly. This is why most
private computer networks are homogeneous systems where all host
computers belong to the same family.

1.1.1.3. Systems for distributed processing

In this section we consider systems in which the processing of a given task is not limited to one host computer, but
distributed over several computers at different locations.

One principle of distributed processing is to do the
processing where the data is. Since the data usually enters the
system at many different locations, this means that the data

processing is distributed. Examples of this principle are local text editing, and validation of data entry close to the terminal. In the case of a distributed data base, i.e. a data base with data stored at different locations, a query may give rise to searches through the stored data at several locations. Again, the processing is done where the data is. This principle leads to a reduction of the data communications traffic, since data processing usually involves data reduction.

A second principle of distributed processing is redundancy. Since the processing is performed at several locations, it is often not too difficult to organize the system such that the different processing centers can replace one another in performing the required work. This leads to very resilient systems characterized by "graceful degradation" in the case of failures, which means that the failure of a processing center does not imply a failure of the overall system, but only results in a reduced processing capacity.

A third principle that can be applied to distributed processing is the construction of dedicated systems. Instead of using a general purpose computer system for executing a variety of necessary tasks, the different components of a distributed processing system could each be specialized to do a particular task. This simplifies the design of each component. Note that this is a very important consideration since complexity means high development costs, software errors and high maintenance costs.

At the time of writing, the field of distributed processing cannot be considered as being well understood. In the following we give some points for illustration.

(a) A distributed algorithm

Consider the problem of finding a strategy for routing data packets through a transmission sub-network from the source to the destination node. We suppose that the packet contains a field indicating the destination node. Each node has a so-called routing table which indicates, for each destination node, the next inter-node circuit over which the packet should be sent. How can the routing tables be established ?

A centralized approach to this problem is possible. It consists of collecting at a given node, or at the network control center, the necessary information, including present failures of nodes and inter-node circuits, queuing delays over the operational circuits, etc. Based on this information, relatively optimized routing tables can be calculated by a relatively complex algorithm, and the results are subsequently sent to all operational nodes for updating the tables. To adapt to the changing environment, this algorithm should be executed as often as possible.

A distributed algorithm was first adopted in the Arpanet[12], and similar algorithms have subsequently been used in many other networks. Again, the routing tables must be updated as often as possible. For each update, the new table values are calculated at each node separately, using the previous table values and information obtained from the immediately neighbouring nodes. Since the calculations of each node are not based on a global knowledge of the network, but only on information about the immediately surrounding region, the resulting tables are clearly not as optimal as centrally determined tables can be. We note, however, the following advantages of the distributed approach :

(1) The algorithm executed at each node is very simple.

(2) Less control packets have to be exchanged.

(3) The complexity of the calculation is independent of the network topology and size.

(4) The danger that the control center of a centralized system may fail is eliminated. The failure of a node is automatically dealt with by the distributed nature of the algorithm.

We note that the routing problem for data networks is one of the few areas for which distributed algorithms have been studied extensively[13]. For most other applications, very few distributed algorithms are known.

(b) Distributed data bases

Following the first principle mentioned above, different parts of a data base are often located at different processing locations. For example, the data base of a bank may be distributed over several centers in different cities, where each center contains the data base information on the clients in that geographical area. Then most transactions can be processed locally.

In other cases, the same information may be contained in several redundant copies at different locations. This has the advantage that the different copies can be used as back-ups for one another. For the information needed frequently at many places, an access to the closest copy reduces the communication costs. Finally, complicated queries may be processed in parallel at several locations, which may reduce the response time.

The above considerations give some reasons for distributing data bases over several locations. Such a distribution introduces many problems for which, at present, practical solutions have been found for some, but not all.

1.1.2.   *Locally distributed systems*

In contrast to the systems considered above, involving
long distance data communications, usually over public data transmission facilities, we consider in this section systems using local data transmission facilities, often privately owned, and suitable for distances up to about one hundred meters. Over such
distances, high speed transmission facilities can be built relatively cheaply, which allows for a closer integration of the different components of the distributed system. We note that similar
transmission facilities are available over long distances, too,
but at a greater cost.

The reasons for distributing the processing in a local
system over several components are those outlined in section
1.1.1.3 : processing where the data is, increasing system reliability and availability by redundancy, and specialization of the
components. The last reason seems to be the most important for
locally distributed systems. Instead of sharing a central processing unit between the different activities to be performed by the
system, relatively independent processing units are provided for
each of these activities. This allows for a simple design for each
processing unit and their optimization, taking advantage of their
specialization.

Typical examples of locally distributed systems are those
derived from centralized computer systems by the addition of specialized mini-computers. Figure 1.4 shows a computer system with
distinct communications and data base processors. The former im-
plements the protocols to be followed for the communication with
distant terminals and other computers over dedicated circuits and
a network, and the latter manages a data base and processes logical requests for enquiry and update. This approach of separating
certain functions of an operating system and implementing them
on a distinct processor can be pushed further. It leads to a computing system consisting of a number of mini- or micro-computers

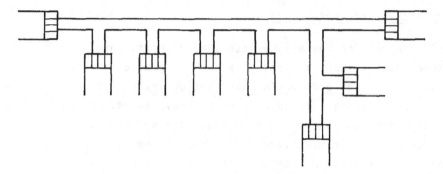

FIGURE 1.5: Shared bus

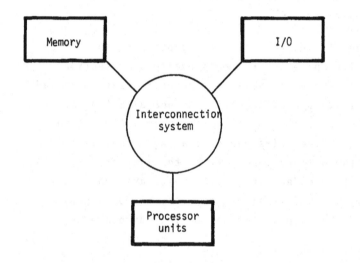

FIGURE 1.6: Basic multiprocessor organisation

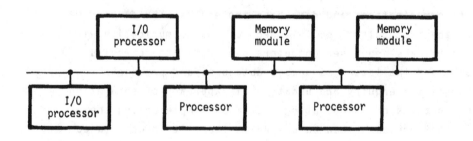

FIGURE 1.7: Time-shared common bus system organization - single bus.

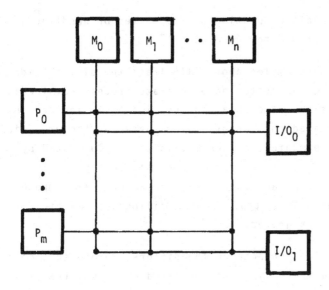

FIGURE 1.8: Crossbar (nonblocking) switch system organisation

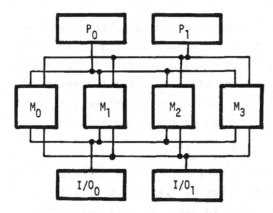

FIGURE 1.9: Multiport-memory system organization - basic organization

each realizing a specific function of the system or handling a
specific input-output or storage device.[14]

Whereas the examples above illustrate the distribution
of activities of a given system onto separate processors, locally
distributed systems are also obtained when initially independent
elements are integrated into an organized system by the provision
of an appropriate communication scheme. This is illustrated by
certain systems for real-time process control, and by systems for
office automation where each person may use a personal computer,
and intelligent terminals, typewriters, filing systems etc. are
interconnected and integrated.

The communication between the different processors of a
locally distributed system is often realized by a data transmissioı
"bus". It consists of one ("sequential bus") or several ("parallel
bus") signaling circuits shared between the communicating processors, as shown in figure 1.5. All connected processors see the
same signals on the bus. Therefore it is important to avoid con-
flicting write accesses to the bus by different processors. This
is the reason for introducing an appropriate discipline for sharing the bus, called the bus access protocol.

There are two basic approaches to the sharing of a bus :
centralized control and distributed control. In the case of centralized control, one of the connected processors is identified
as the bus controller, or primary station, and all other processors play a secondary role. The latter are not allowed to write
on the bus, unless they are invited by the primary to do so, i.e.
unless they are "polled".

If all connected processors are to have the same rights
to the use of the bus, either a centralized bus controller is
added which polls all processors in turn, or a distributed bus
control is implemented in the processors. In the latter case,

"contention" may occur, when several processors try to write on the bus simultaneously. Therefore a distributed bus protocol has to detect contention and recover from it. Contention can usually be detected by the processors involved, which listen to the bus signals and recognize interference with another processor when the signal read is inconsistant with the signal written. Recovery is usually performed by a retry after some delay. Indefinite cycling through reties and consecutive interferences must be avoided, for example by using randomly chosen delays.[15]

The details of the bus access protocols vary considerably between different systems. Most systems use a mixture of the centralized and distributed approaches. For example, the input-output channel interface of a computer system is usually a parallel bus over which several device control units transmit data in an order determined by the channel processor which acts as bus controller. But there is contention of the data ready signals (usually involving interrupts) from the devices which can be resolved by a priority scheme between the devices. Another example is the provision of several processors that could play the role of the centralized bus controller. At any given time, only one of them would play the primary role of the controller, whereas the others would act as secondaries. However any of them could take over the primary role after being invited to do so by the acting primary[16], or when the latter has a failure.

In the case of very high transmission capacities and/or longer distances, the propagation delay of the signals over the bus can no longer be neglected. If refection of the propagating signals at the terminations of the circuits is avoided, one obtains a so-called multi-point circuit. Except for noticable transmission delays, it has the same characteristics as a bus. A similar transmission facility is also provided by terrestrial and satellite radio transmission. All these facilities have in common the provision of information broadcasted between all connected components,

and the same principles apply to the sharing of the transmission
facility.

1.1.3. *Multi-processor systems*

Multi-processor systems are computer systems consisting
of several closely coupled processors. The basic organization, as
shown in figure 1.6, involves processors, and input-output (I/0)
processors that access memory units through some kind of interconnection system. The memory units represent the central memory
of the system, and in many cases the memory access is provided by
a shared memory bus, as shown in figure 1.7. Other possible schemes for interconnection are a crossbar switch matrix (see figure
1.8)and an organization with multi-port memories (see figure
1.9).[17]

Reasons for introducing multiple processors into a computer system are the same as for the distribution of processing
(see section 1.1.2). An additional objective is increased system
performance.

Communication between the processes run on the different
processors of a multi-processor system is usually realized through
the access of shared memory. In this system organization, the access of memory units containing private data of a given process
involves the same hardware functions as the access to shared memory used for interprocess communication. Therefore this organization allows for very close coupling between the different processes of the system.

1.1.4. *Virtual distribution*

We call "virtual distribution of control and data" the
introduction of conceptually independent processes within a system whose physical realization does not correspond to this con-
ceptual organization. A typical example of virtual distribution

is an operating system, for a single processor computer, which is
designed as a collection of processes, each performing a particular task and interacting through a given communication mecanism.
The system software is usually structured into several hierarchical layers, where the first layer (directly on the hardware level)
provides the multiplexing of the available (hardware) processors
among the processes of the system and the inter-process communication mecanism. If the adopted interprocess communication mecanism
resembles a message system, the overall system design may easily
be adapted to a physically distributed system.[18]

The main reason for the distribution of processing between several virtual processes is to obtain a modular system design.[19] The introduction of a process for each activity in the
system seems to simplify the overall system design and to lead to
simple interaction between the different parts of the system.

Since virtual distribution is realized through software
support, the communication mecanism provided to realize the interaction between the different system components may be adapted to
particular requirements. As a consequence, this mecanism varies
considerably from one system to another. Certain primitives for
inter-process communications have been incorporated into system
programming languages. The following list presents the most important concepts.

(a) Process creation :

- coroutines,[20]
- static declarations of parallel processes,[21]
- fork and join primitives for evoking parallel execution of
  statements,[22]
- dynamic process creation and management, possibly with hierarchical inter-process dependencies[23] (a "father" process crea-
  tes and supervises its "son" processes).

(b) Mutual exclusion[24]

- critical regions for accessing shared variables,
- conditional critical regions.

(c) Explicit process scheduling

- semaphores,[25]
- event signaling and waiting.[26]

(d) Message queues

- fixed message queues between pairs of processes,[27]
- mailboxes, one for each process,[28]
- exchange of command-response messages.[29]

1.2. CLASSIFICATION OF DISTRIBUTED SYSTEMS

Distributed systems may be classified according to many different aspects. In the following we consider four aspects that seem particularly useful for a classification of distributed systems. We base our discussion on a system model consisting of several system components which interact through some communication mecanism, as shown in figure 1.10.

1.2.1. Degree of coupling

The degree of coupling between two system components may be defined informally as the ratio between the amount of data exchanged between these components per amount of local processing performed. Taking the degree of coupling as a criterion for a classification leads to the distinction between the following kinds of systems :

(a) systems with weak coupling between components, typically using communication channels of some Kbits per second, sometimes cal led "thin wire communication",

(b) distributed systems with strong coupling, typically using a
communication channel with a capacity comparable with the
transfer rate of secondary storage devices,

(c) very strongly coupled systems, for which data transfer between
components is nearly as efficient as access by a component to
the data it processes.

We note that this classification underlies the distinction, made
in section 1.1, between (a) systems distributed over long distance, (b) locally distributed systems, and (c) multi-processor and
virtually distributed systems.

1.2.2. *Interconnection structure*

Whereas the classification aspect above involves mainly
the transmission capacity of the communication mecanism, the classification according to the interconnection structure involves its
logical structure, and in particular the addressing and routing
strategies.

The following interconnection structures may be distinguished :[30]

(a) Direct interconnections between components :

(a1) Dedicated facility for each pair of communicating components : Typical examples are complete interconnection
structures as shown in figure 1.11, and loop structures[31]
as shown in figure 1.12.

(a2) Communications facility shared between all components :
Typical examples are local bus structures, as shown in
figure 1.5, or radio broadcast channels. In contrast to
the structures of (a1), contention among the system components must be resolved. Shared memory of multi-processor systems can also be considered in this category.

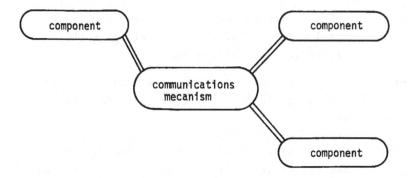

FIGURE 1.10: Communications mecanism and its users

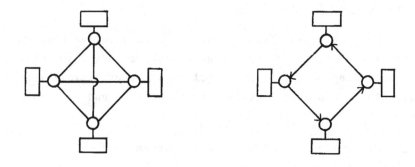

FIGURE 1.11: Complete interconnection   FIGURE 1.12: Loop connection
            structure   structure

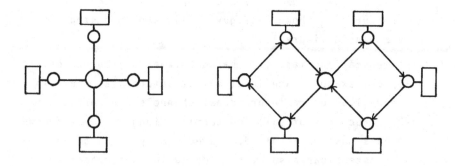

FIGURE 1.13: Star-like interconnection structures

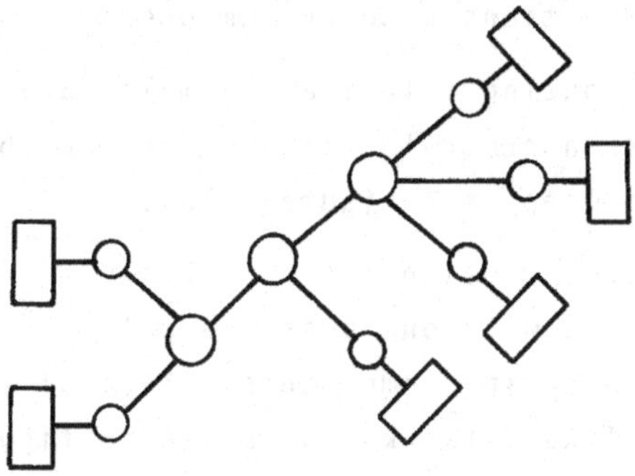

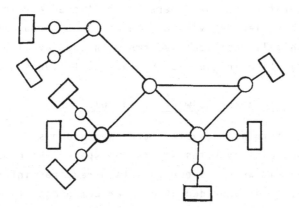

FIGURE 1.14: Tree-like interconnection structure

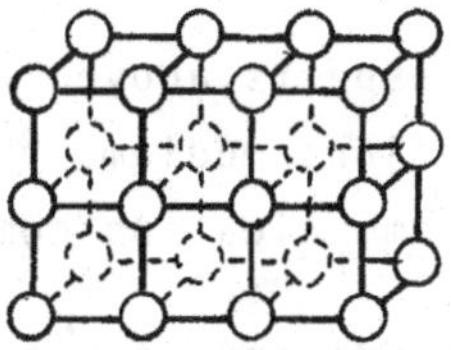

FIGURE 1.15: n-cube interconnection structure (n = 3)

FIGURE 1.16: Irregular interconnection structure

(b) Indirect interconnections between components :

    (b1) Centralized routing : Typical examples are star-like
        networks with a central switch where each branch may
        consist of a loop (see figure 1.13).

    (b2) Non-centralized routing :
        (b2i)   Networks with one possible path per pair of
               communicating components : Typical examples are
               tree-like networks, as shown in figure 1.14.
        (b2ii) Networks with generally several possible commu-
               nication paths between two components : Typical
               examples are networks connected as an n-cube
               (see figure 1.15), or irregular networks.

1.2.3.   *Interdependence of components*

Whereas the classification aspects above involve mainly
the characteristics of the communications medium, the following
two depend on the structure of the communicating components.

Components are strongly interdependent when the operation
of one component relies on the successful operation of the other
component(s). On the contrary, components are weakly interdependent when the failure of one component does not jeopardize the
successful operation of the others. As mentioned earlier (section
1.1.1.2), such system behavior may be obtained through redundancy,
and leads to highly resilient systems with good availability and
graceful degradation in the case of partial failures.

1.2.4.   *Synchronization between components*

Most distributed systems are asynchronous, in the sense
that each components operates at its own speed (which may vary in
time) and may wait when its own operation requires information not
yet available, to be provided by another component. The speed of

the overall system is determined by the speed of the slowest compo
nent. For such an asynchronous system, the communication mecanism
has to provide a "pacing" or "flow control" facility for correla-
ting the effective processing speeds of the different components.

Some other distributed systems are synchronous, in the
sense that there is a fixed relation between the processing speeds
of the different components. The synchronization between the components is maintained by a common clock, which is usually provided
through the communication medium.

1.3. DEFINITION OF "DISTRIBUTED SYSTEM"

We consider a "distributed system" as consisting of several interacting components, as shown in figure 1.10. The degree of
coupling between the components may be weak or strong, but very
strongly coupled systems, such as multi-processor systems, are
excluded. All kinds of interconnection structures are considered.
We are particularly interested in systems with weakly interdependent components, and in questions of compatibility which must be
considered if a given component is to be replaced by another component, or one component is to communicate with a large number of
different components.

We also include in our definition, virtually distributed
systems, i.e. systems designed with an internal structure which
would allow for a distribution of functions over several physically disjoint components, but actually implemented on one physical
component.

We hope to demonstrate in the following chapters that
distributed systems may be designed using a specification method
which is equally suitable for physically distributed implementation as for centralized implementation in one physical component.
Given such a system design, it is a matter of cost and efficiency

to choose the best physical distribution of functions[32] ; and this choice should be independent of the design of the logical system components.

FOOTNOTES

1. See for example [Davi 73], chapters 2 and 4.

2. Typical applications and characteristics of terminals which
   are used in remote access to computers are described in
   [Hobb 72].

3. See for example [Davi 73], chapter 7.

4. See for example [Doll 72].

5. Statistical multiplexing in data networks is an instance of
   resource sharing. The problems and solutions adopted are
   similar to those encountered in resource sharing in computer
   operating systems (see for example [Klei 75] or [Coff 73]).
   The consideration of queuing delays is crucial for the optimization of the transmission network, taking into account
   the network cost and the expected transmission delays.

6. See for example [Kahn 72] where possible applications for
   and usage of the Arpanet are described.

7. Funded by the Advanced Research Projects Agency (ARPA) of the
   US National Defence Department, the Arpanet was the first
   large scale experience with packet-switched data transmission
   Still operational, it allows resource sharing between a large
   number of computer centers in universities and research centers. The main objectives and characteristics are described
   in [Robe 70].

8. Building on the experience gained with the Arpanet, the
   Cyclades network has much contributed to the state of the art
   of packet-switched data communications. Its major features
   are described in [Pouz 73].

9. The following packet-switched transmission services have
    been defined, to be provided by public data networks :
    (a) virtual circuits and (b) datagrams. For virtual circuits,
    a virtual connection must be established before packets can
    be exchanged, whereas datagrams are selfsufficient packets,
    including complete addressing information, which are sent
    independently of one another. The internal operation of a
    packet-switched network does not necessarily reflect these
    characteristics of the provided transmission services
    [Kirs 76].

10. An overview of the issues of standardization in data commu-
    nications is given in [Boch 77c]. For a status report see
    [Cott 77].

11. Different approaches to this problem are discussed in
    [Gerl 73].

12. See for example [Gerl 73].

13. The particular aspect of avoiding loops, which could be in-
    troduced by a distributed algorithm using local information
    only, is considered in [Nayl 75] and [Merl 77].

14. See for example [Prob 77].

15. The design principles of a high-speed, sequential bus with
    distributed control for applications in office automation
    and distributed processing are given in [Metc 76]. A similar
    bus discipline is described in [Somm 76].

16. A bus discipline for a parallel bus with possibly several
    alternating primary processors is examplified by the IEEE
    standard 488 (originally Hewlett-Packard [Knob 75]).

17. A more detailed discussion of multiprocessor systems can be
    found in [Ensl 77].

18. The design of a computer operating system based on parallel processes communicating through the exchange of messages is described, for example, in [Brin 70]. "Message driven" processes were adopted for the software design of the public data network Datapac [DATAPAC] as described in [Mell 77] and [Cunn 77]. The network system is implemented on several geographically distributed special-purpose multi-processor systems.

19. [Horn 73] describes a formalized concept of "processes" which is used for structuring complex systems into simpler modules.

20. Coroutines are provided by Simula. See for example [Dahl 72]

21. As for example in Concurrent Pascal [Brin 75] and Modula [Wirt 77b]

22. See for example in [Karp 69].

23. See for example [Sevc 72], [Cunn 77], or [Jamm 77]. Hierarchical process dependencies in a distributed environment are discussed in [Mart 77].

24. See for example [Brin 73], sections 3.3 and 3.4.

25. See for example [Dijk 68].

26. Semaphores can be used for explicit scheduling. The combination of shared variables with mutually exclusive access through a predetermined set of procedures, together with event queues for explicit scheduling of processes has been called a monitor (see for example [Hoar 74]).

27. See for example [Kahn 74] or [Ridd 72].

28. See for example [Brin 70],

29. See for example [Goos 72].

30. A similar classification is proposed in [Aude 75].

31. See for example [Ande 75].

32. Some method for optimizing the distribution of system
     functions over several physically distinct components are
     discussed in [Jenn 77].

CHAPTER II

PARALLELISM

What is the meaning of "parallism" and "parallel" when
applied to processes ? The origin of these terms lies outside
the field of computer science. Parallel processes are found in
the world for which the computer analysts build application systems or simulation models. The mastery of system complexity is
closely related to the concept of parallelism. The scope of a
process within a system depends on the level of abstraction from
which the system is considered, and the more the processes are
independent of one another the more decomposition of a system
into parallel processes is useful.

2.1. PARALLEL PROCESSES AND APPLICATIONS

By now it is common place to consider data processing and
other computer application systems, as a collection of communicating parallel processes. This is by analogy to many biological,
social and industrial systems, which have a much longer history.
It is not clear whether this similarity stems from the human inability to think in terms different from those he is used to, or
is an indication that these concepts are essential to the building complex systems. In many cases, the processes within a computer application system are related to the processes of the environment for which the computer system is built. As examples, we
may consider interactive systems, real-time control systems, and
simulation systems.

In the case of interactive systems, the system's environment
consists essentially of the human users that communicate with the
system through terminals. Typical examples are the computing facility of a software house or university, an interactively used

data base, computer aided instruction and learning, or real-time control of complex systems by humans, such as pilots, etc. Usually, in each of these applications, many operators use the same system. As shown in figure 2.1, the system usually contains at least two processes for each human user : (i) a "user process", usually implemented in a "host computer", which is responsible for executing the operations the user wants to the system to perform, and (ii) a "terminal process", often implemented in an intelligent terminal, which is responsible for the communication with the user, via displays, keyboards and other devices suitable for human interaction, and for converting this communication into a form suitable to the user process.

In the case of a real-time control system, the environment consists essentially of the physical devices to be controlled. In the particular case of a computer's operating system, these devices are disks, tape units, printers, interactive terminals, as well as central memory and processing units. Other examples are systems for data acquisition and supervision of scientific experiments, space flights, etc., or industrial systems for verifying the quality of manufactured products or for supervising an automated production. process. Sometimes the environment covered is widely distributed, as for instance for systems supervising pipelines. As shown in figure 2.2, the control system usually contains one process associated directly with each external device controlled, or group of devices which logically form an external process. Within the control system, which may contain other processes as well, these processes "represent" the external devices they are associated with, and they communicate with the latter by appropriate input-output devices, often involving digital-analogue conversion.

In the case of simulation systems, it is natural to represent each physical process to be simulated by a simulating process in the simulation system. In addition, the system will contain processes for supervising the simulation process and obtaining the desired results. An example is shown in figure 2.3, which represents a manufacturing process, where some raw material, stored in P_7, is used by the processes P_1 through P_5 to build semi-finished products, which are stored in P_8, P_9 and P_{10} respectively, and which are assembled by process P_6 into two types of finished products and one type of defective product. The storing processes, P_7 through P_{10}, are of a particular type. Except for possible product degradation during storage, they may be considered passive processes, exchanging products with the other processes P_1 through P_6, considered active.

We note in closing that the term "process" is different from the term "processor". The latter is applied to the hardware device which makes the execution of processes possible. Usually, a given processor is responsible for executing several (logical) processes, sometimes in collaboration with other processors.

2.2. CONSTRAINTS ON INDEPENDENCE

Different processes within a given system are usually considered as being relatively independent of one another. Complete independence is usually excluded, because it would lead to unrelated subsystems. Usually, the different processes are considered independent of one another[1] except for certain explicitely introduced dependencies. Different kinds of process interdependencies may be considered ; they are usually related to the mutual exclusion of several processes during the access of shared resources, or to process cooperation involving the exchange of data.

If several processes access a shared resource which may only be accessed by one process at a time, it may occasionally be necessary to delay any processes that want to access the resource, when it is being accessed by another process. As an example, we assume that the processes P_2 and P_3 of figure 2.3 share a common tool for their operation so that they may have to wait for one another. If the processing time of P_2 and P_3 is short compared to

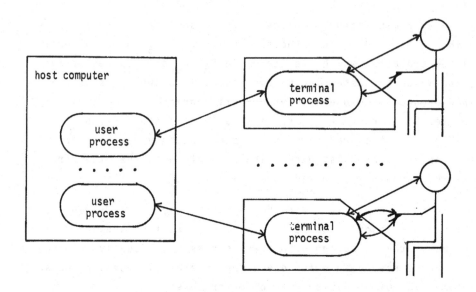

FIGURE 2.1: Processes in a computer application system

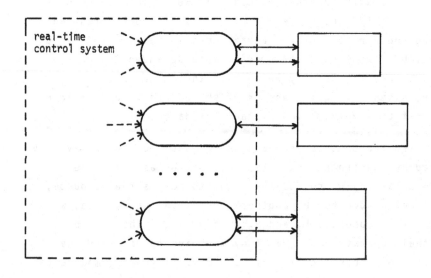

Figure 2.2: Processes in a real-time control system

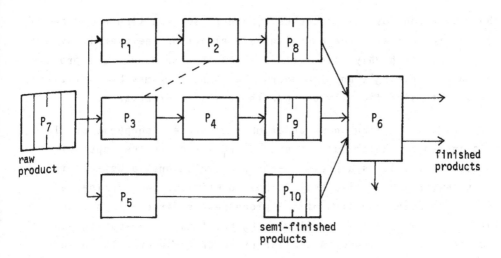

FIGURE 2.3: Processes in a manufacturing plant

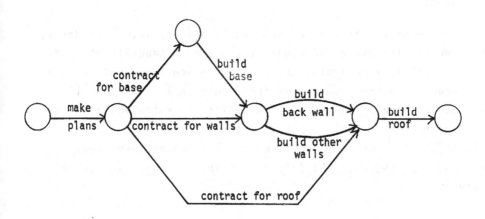

FIGURE 2.4: Example of PERT scheduling

the time needed by the processes P_1 and P_4 such waiting would be
very infrequent and have a negligeable effect on the overall system
operation. For highly used resources, on the contrary, many processes may be waiting[2], and the average waiting time may be sufficiently long to significantly degrade the overall performance.

Figure 2.3 also shows an example of process cooperation. In
this instance, the product of process P_1 serves as the input of
process P_2 . This is a producer-consumer relationship between two
processes, which implies that P_2 has to wait for the termination
of P_1 . Here the coupling of the processes is direct : since no
intermediate storage is available, P_2 has to start executing as
soon as P_1 has finished. A similar producer-consumer relationship
exists between P_2 and P_6 , except that the intermediate storage
process P_8 allows for a certain time lag between the two processes.
Other examples of process cooperation, also involving a sequence
in which certain operations must be executed, are given by the
PERT project scheduling method (see figure 2.4), or by systems in
which the different processes communicate through the exchange of
messages, where, clearly, the message reception always comes after
the sending.

The synchronization rules implied by process interdependency,
such as mutual exclusion and cooperation, are in general not sufficient to completely determine the relative execution speed and order between the processes of a system. Additional synchronization
decisions are usually taken by a scheduling algorithm which, in a
sense, supervises the whole system. This algorithm has to avoid
deadlocks[3], where several processes wait upon each other, thus
preventing any progress, and insure that the schedule is fair for
all processes.

2.3. MODULAR SYSTEM STRUCTURE AND ABSTRACTION

Most systems are too complex to be understood as a whole
by the human mind. Therefore, it is necessary to introduce a structure subdividing a system into several more or less independent
subsystems, processes[4], or modules. Such a structure allows each
subsystem to be understood individually, the interaction of the
subsystems leading to the understanding of the system as a whole.

The interaction between the subsystems is related to their
interdependency and may be characterized by the assumptions each
given subsystem must make about its environment, i.e. the other
subsystems. As discussed in section 2.2, three levels of inter-
dependence may be distinguished :

(a) No interaction between certain subsystems, such as for
     processes P_1, P_4 and P_5 in figure 2.3, i.e. no interdepen-
     dence.

(b) Implicite interaction between certain subsystems due to
     scheduling constraints for shared resources. This interaction
     is not explicitely visible to the subsystems involved, but
     may nevertheless influence their operation[5].

(c) Explicit interaction involving cooperation between a certain
     number of subsystems. This kind of interaction usually invol-
     ves the exchange of messages and/or one subsystem performing
     work for another one. This necessitates agreement on the
     meaning of the messages or procedure parameters exchanged
     between the subsystems.

A basic design principle favors a system structure with infrequent and simple subsystem interactions. The "interface" between
two interacting subsystems may be defined as the set of assumptions
each subsystem must make about the operation of the other. Such an
interface must specify what each subsystem does, as seen from the
outside, but not (necessarily) how[6].

Complementary to the division of a system into subsystems is the abstraction which consists of considering the collection of subsystems with their interactions as a whole, ignoring the subsystem structure, and considering the interaction of this system with its environment. For example, figure 2.5 shows a structure of subsystems which realizes process P_6 of figure 2.3. In figure 2.3 abstraction is made from the details of P_6's structure shown in figure 2.5. If the interface of P_6 with its environment is well defined, the internal structure of P_6 , as shown in figure 2.5, is irrelevant to the operation of the whole system, as shown in figure 2.3.

Clearly, system subdivision or abstraction may be performed at several levels as indicated in figure 2.6, giving rise to a hierarchy of system descriptions. This principle is not only useful for the design of computer systems[7], but also for the understanding of complex biological and social systems[8]. It is important to note that the amount of parallel activity found in any given system depends on the level of detail (or abstraction) on which the system is considered. For example in figure 2.3, the operation of process P_6 is considered as a whole (no parallelism), whereas the consideration of figure 2.5 introduces some parallel activity between the subsystems of the process. Another example is shown in figure 2.7, where different levels of detail (or abstraction) are considered for the query handling process of an interactive data base.

It follows from the above considerations that the understanding of a system at different levels of details (or abstraction) is a basic tool for the design of complex systems. This aspect of system design should be supported by the system specification method (or programming language) used during the design[9] .

FIGURE 2.5: A more detailed description of process P_6 of figure 2.3

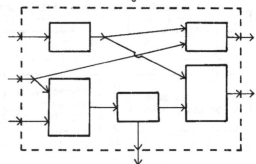

FIGURE 2.6: A given system specified in three different levels of details (or abstraction)

Explanations:

↑ abstraction
¦ (less details)
¦
¦
↓ subdivision
(more details)

↑ interaction between subsystems
↓

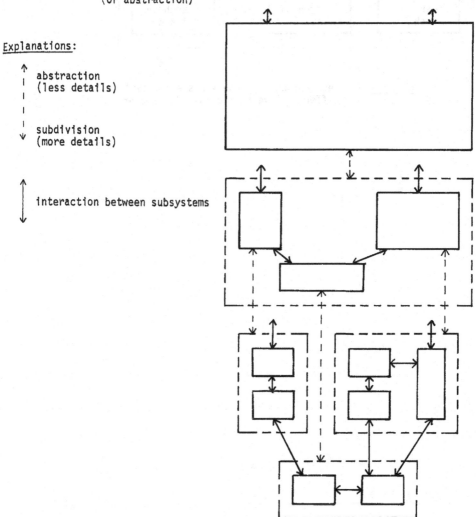

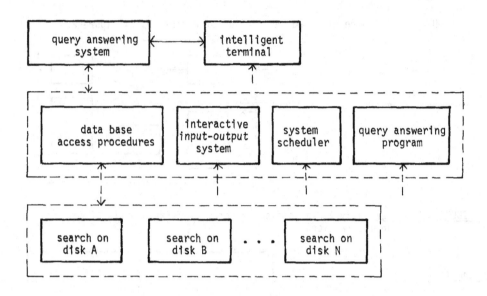

FIGURE 2.7: Description of a query answering system in
different levels of detail (incomplete)

FOOTNOTES

1. The use of independent processes in the programming of
   operating systems is discussed in [Brin 73], section 3.

2. Processes waiting for a resource are usually organized in
   a queue. Sometimes several queues, corresponding to different service priorities, are associated with a resource.
   The queuing analysis of such systems is important for determining the overall performance of the system. See for example [Klei 75].

3. See for example [Coff 73], section 2.3.

4. Some examples of operating systems structured as a collection
   of several processes are described in [Brin 70] and [Mell 77]
   Structuring principles based on the concept of processes are
   described in [Horn 73].

5. Implicit interaction also leads to protection problems, as
   exemplified by information leak through so-called covered
   channels [Lamp 73].

6. See for example [Parn 77].

7. See for example [Dijk 68b]. The concept of nearly completely
   decomposable systems has also been explained in [Cour 77]
   and applied to performance analysis.

8. [Simo 62].

9. The concepts of *class* [Dahl 72] or abstract data types
   [Lisk 75] are provided in certain programming languages for
   providing a means for abstraction. A language construct for
   hierarchical process structures would also be useful.

CHAPTER III

COMMON PROBLEMS

This chapter reviews some well-known problem areas encountered during the design of a computer application system. These problems are not specific to distributed systems. They were first studied in the framework of single processor computer systems, their operating systems, and application programs. However, some of the solutions to these problems are specific to distributed systems. Without claiming complete coverage of the subject, this chapter presents some example problems and a few possible solutions

We believe that these problems should not be considered independently of one another, but a system design method, or particular system design should be chosen such that all these problems are solved, in so far as possible, simultaneously by the same approach, tool or mecanism. In this chapter, the problems are presented separately in order to simplify the discussion. In the following chapters, several system specification methods are presented which should be considered with a view to solving these problems.

3.1. COOPERATION

3.1.1. Compatibility

Cooperation between several system components is only possible if the interfaces of the components are compatible. There are two levels of compatibility :

(a) If <u>functional compatibility</u> does not exist, cooperation is not possible. Consider for example a standard alpha-numeric terminal to be used for displaying arabic text, or a 6 Mbyte disk to store a 60 million character text file.

(b) If <u>procedural compatibility</u> does not exist, but the components are functionally compatible, cooperation can only be obtained by introducing a suitable adaptation module which translates between the communication procedures used by the different components. For example, alpha-numeric text can be translated between different character codes, or virtual circuit data communication can be operated through the X.25 or an HDLC interface.[1]

3.1.2. *Synchronization*

An example of a synchronous system is an assembly line where all workers work at the same speed. An example of an asynchronous system is a job shop where different processes work at independent speeds and semi-finished products are stored between the different steps of the processing.

3.2. *DISTRIBUTED RESOURCE SHARING*

Resource sharing is one of the main problems in the design of computer operating systems. Most resources impose restrictions (for example mutual exclusion) as to when they can be accessed by the different processes in the system. Scheduling algorithms have to maintain these restrictions for each resource. Such algorithms have been extensively studied for a centralized environment, where the scheduling decisions for the whole system are made by a centralized scheduler.

For a distributed system, the following three approaches may be taken :

(a) <u>centralized scheduling</u> : one component, the scheduler, is responsible for scheduling all resources in the system ;

(b) <u>scheduling at the resource</u> : a scheduling module is associated with each sharable resource. It processes requests for resource access coming from all components of the system ;

(c) <u>distributed scheduling algorithm for a given resource</u> : all
processes competing for a resource execute a distributed algorithm
which determines the schedule.

Considering only one resource, the approaches (a) and (b)
are quite similar. However, the avoidance of deadlocks in the presence of several resources, seems to be more difficult in the case
of approach (b).[2]

The approach (c) seems to be appropriate if the resource
is not localized in one component, so that approach (b) is not
applicable.[3]

3.3.   NAMING AND ADDRESSING

The following examples demonstrate the wide variety of
naming and addressing problems and approaches to their solution.

3.3.1. Search strategies for link editors

Each link editor or operating system has a strategy for
identifying and locating object program modules to satisfy the
external references of a load module. Given a reference name, such
a strategy finds, if possible, a corresponding program module by
searching through the provided input file, private object files,
public program libraries and execution support modules. This is
analogous to an addressing scheme.

3.3.2. Naming of input-output flows

A given input or output flow, for example the input character stream from an interactive terminal to the application program in a computer system is identified in many different ways,
depending on the frame of reference within the system structure.
For instance from the point of view of the terminal driver, the
terminal is usually identified by an integer value, sometimes

called the I/O address, and usually a physically fixed value. For
the scheduler of the operating system, the input stream could be
identified by a port number associated with the application program, or the address in central memory of a file control block
which contains the control information of the stream. For the
control command interpreter, the input stream is usually characterized by a file name, such as INPUT. The application program,
finally, may use another name, such as USER-TERMINAL, to identify
the same file.

3.3.3. The addressing scheme of telephone networks

The addressing scheme of telephone networks is hierarchical, as shown in figure 3.1. In the case that the different telephone sets of an organization share the access to the public network, each telephone set is identified by an internal number within
the range of the office exchange. The office exchange is identified
by a local number within the range of the local telephone exchange,
etc. For establishing a connection with a telephone set connected
to the same office exchange, dialling the internal number is sufficient, as shown in figure 3.2a. To establish a connection outside
the range of the office exchange, the dialling sequence must start
with a local escape number which is interpreted as such by the office exchange of the originating party. An example of long distance
dialling is shown in figure 3.2b .

3.3.4. Process addressing by ports

Like a telephone set on a public telephone network, a computer system connected to a data network is usually identified by
a number which identifies the link between the network and the computer, i.e. its address. In order to distinguish between the different processes, within the computer system, that communicate with
other processes or terminals through the network, the concept of
ports has been proposed.[4] Each process has a certain number of

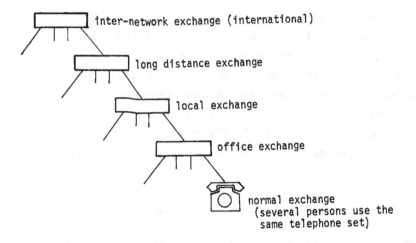

FIGURE 3.1: Hierarchical addressing scheme of telephone networks

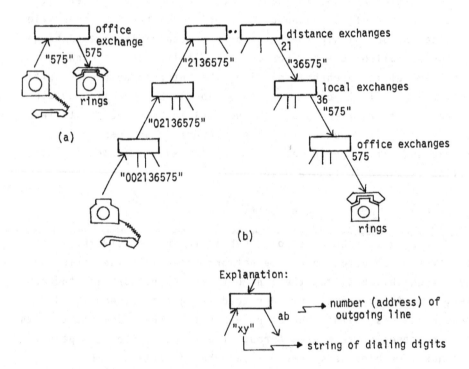

FIGURE 3.2: Telephone call establishment and addressing information

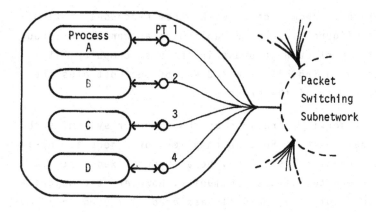

FIGURE 3.3: A Transport Station is a collection of Ports

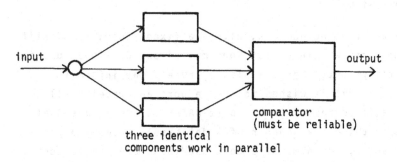

FIGURE 3.4: Reliability obtained through hardware redundance

A fault-tolerant sort program

ensure sorted (S) ∧ (sum(S) = sum(prior S))
by quickersort (S)
else by quicksort (S)
else error

Note: Rather than incur the cost
of checking that the elements are a permutation of
the original items, it merely requires the sum of the
elements to remain the same.

FIGURE 3.5: Example of a recovery block

ports through which it communicates with other processes or terminals, as shown in figure 3.3. For establishing a connection through
the network with a particular process in the host computer, it is
therefore necessary to indicate the address of the host plus the
appropriate port number of the process.

Well known services provided by the computer system, such
as a particular data base, a Fortran compiler, or a general log-in
facility to the operating system, may be assigned fixed port numbers, which are known to the user community. However, the majority
of port numbers may not be permanently assigned, but used on a tem-
porary basis by the user created processes. The available ports
(or port numbers) are shared among the processes that reside in
the computer system.

Instead of using numbers, within a fixed range, to identify
the available ports within a host, one may allow for alpha-numeric
names to identify ports. For example, a process may inform the
operating system that it wishes to open a port and receive all
incoming messages addressed to the port DATABASE (we assume that
this process is the query manager of a database). Except for the
"well known" ports, the name of a port used by a process for communication may be changed dynamically by the latter.[5]

Extending the scope of the port names from one host computer to the whole network yields a system where the user, which
communicates with a given port name, need not be aware of the physical location of the process which serves this port.[6]

3.4. PROTECTION

We consider here the protection of system integrity against
hardware faults and software bugs, as well as inadvertant users
and those persons that try to obtain information they are not sup-
posed to obtain. It is important to distinguish between the mecanisms that provide this protection and the security policy

implemented in the system which determines the access rights and capabilities of the different processes and users.[7] The following points provide protection mecanisms :

(a) A modular system design using extended type objects as system modules, combined with small protection domains placed around these modules prevents unanticipated or undesirable actions of a module from disturbing other parts of the system.[8]

(b) The distribution of the different system modules onto several physically disjoint components increases the independence between the modules and eliminates unwanted interferences between the modules.[9]

(c) Physical control over the hardware of the system is a means of avoiding physical infractions.

(d) Identification of users is a means of protection at the system-user interface. Possible methods are the use of passwords, signatures, identification cards, etc.[10]

(e) Identification of terminals and other physical devices in distributed systems is useful as an additional check on the integrity of the communications medium, and make sure that some remote device has not been replaced by some other unauthorized item.

3.4.1. *Protection in distributed systems*[11]

The physical security (point (c) above) is not always attainable in distributed systems. For example, radio communication channels and circuits for accessing telephone or data networks can be tapped without any impact on the communication channel. It is also possible to falsify the data exchanged, or to introduce additional data into an ongoing exchange, provided the system is well enough known to the intruder. It is therefore impractical to physically secure the privacy and integrity of the information exchanged between distant system components.

A possible approach to protection is the use of encryption. For better protection, encryption may be used independently at different levels in the system. For example, a distributed system using a communication sub-network, independent encryption may be used for each process to process communication, and additionally and independently over each link between a system component and the sub-network.

Most encryption techniques use matching keys at each end of the encrypted communication path.[12] A pair of keys must be agreed upon prior to the communication.[13]

3.5. ERROR RECOVERY[14]

3.5.1. Error detection

Before error recovery can be performed, the occurrence of an error must be detected. Error detection is common practice in data transmission and storage techniques, where error detecting codes are used. The principle is the addition of redundant information which must agree with the original data to be transmitted or stored. During the reception or reading from storage, the consistancy can be checked and possible errors are detected with high probability.

Frequently used error detecting codes are the following :

(a) parity bit : the addition of one redundant bit such that an even (or uneven) parity is obtained for each character or memory word (single bit errors are detected, errors involving an even number of bits are not detected) ;

(b) checksum : the addition, to a block of data, of a redundant octet (or word) containing the modulo sum of all octets (words) of the block ;

(c) longitudinal parity, and

(d) polynomial or cyclic codes : similar to (b) .

The polynomial or cyclic codes present the best error detection characteristics.[15]

For errors involving only a few bits, redundant codes can be used which not only detect possible errors, but are also able to determine the original data, i.e. they are "error correcting codes".

3.5.2. *Recovery by retry*

One of the simplest forms of error recovery is recovery by retry, which consists of reperforming the operation which lead to the error condition. In the case of transmission errors, or read or write errors on magnetic surfaces, the operation will usually perform correctly the second time. A certain number of retries are usually admitted, and failure to perform the operation is declared in the case that none of the retries was successful.

If the error is due to a persistant hardware fault or a software bug, repeated execution of the same operation will usually not change the error condition. For these kinds of errors, the recovery strategy by retry is not appropriate, but one of the strategies described below may be used.

3.5.3. *Redundant hardware*

The provision of redundant hardware makes it possible to recover from hardware faults of a limited nature. Different degrees of redundancy may be foreseen, depending on the desired reliability of the system. In decreasing order of reliability, we mention the following approaches :

(a) Three identical components operate in parallel, as shown in figure 3.4. A majority vote among the three determines the correct result and detects any errors in one component.

(b) Two identical components operate in parallel and any error
of one component is detected by a discrepancy of the results. If
a possible malfunction of one component can be detected by itself,
the other component can be used as stand-by.

(c) Only one component operates, but similar components are available in the case of a failure of the former. Either one component
is identified as the back-up, or several identical components share
the processing load, as long as they are operational.

3.5.4. The design principle of recovery blocks

The concept of recovery blocks has been proposed as a
design principle for building reliable and resilient systems.[16]
It is intended as a method for specifying recovery mecanisms for
software bugs, as well as for spurious or persistant hardware errors. For software bugs, the methods of retry or hardware (and
software) duplication clearly do not work as long as the input
data do not change.

The principle consists of subdividing the system into modules which are the units of error recovery, i.e. the recovery
blocks. For error detection, a verification condition is associated with each module. Depending on the output result parameters
of the module, the condition must be satisfied after each execution of the module. (The presence of such a conditions represents
a certain redundancy in the values of the output parameters). The
verification condition is used to detect errors.

The operation of the module is specified in several (different) program versions. When the module is executed, the first
version is executed and the verification condition is tested. If
it is satisfied, it is assumed that the result is correct and the
execution of the module ends. If it is not satisfied, an error has
occurred and the second program version is executed, which is
followed by another test of the verification condition. If the
program versions are sufficiently different from one another,

there is a good chance that the second version works correctly after the first one failed. If all program versions fail to check the verification condition, then the module, as a whole, is considered to have failed.

It seems that this approach to error recovery is of general applicability. An example is shown in figure 3.5.

3.6.   REAL TIME CONSIDERATIONS

It is useful to distinguish the following three levels of real time constraints[17] :

(a)   No real time constraints :
       termination within finite time : typical for batch applications ;

(b)   Probabilistic real time constraints :
       termination within a given time with a given probability
       (real time constraint on average execution time, but no definite time limit) : typical for real time systems for interactive applications ;

(c)   Real time constraints :
       termination within a definite time limit : typical for applications in process control etc. (real "real time" systems).

Systems with real time constraints are clearly much harder to build than systems with probabilistic or no real time constraints Therefore it seems good practice to design real time systems such that real time constraints apply for as few system modules as possible, and that for the remaining parts of the system only probabilistic constraints apply.

3.6.1. *Time-outs*

A typical application of a time-out mecanism can be found
in most data transmission protocols for recovery after message
loss. If, within a predetermined real time period, the sender does
not receive an acknowledgement for a message sent, the message is
retransmitted. If the time period lapses before the acknowledgement
is received, one says "a time-out occurs".

A time-out period is related to a real time constraint. If,
in the example, the message transmission and reception of an acknowledgement is always executed (except in the case of message loss)
within a definite time limit, there is no problem : the time-out
period will be set longer than this time limit. If, however, there
is no definite, but only a probabilistic time limit for the response,
then for any time-out period chosen, it may happen that the acknowledgement of the original message sent arrives after the time-out
occurred and the message was retransmitted. This possibility may
have implications on the system's design.

3.6.2. *Clock synchronization in distributed systems*

For distributed systems with real time constraints it seems
necessary to define a global real time which is known to all system
components, and represents the physical time. If each component
uses its own clock, there must be some algorithm for synchronizing
the different clocks.[18]

Much simplicity is gained for the system if no global real
time is needed. For many distributed real time applications, it is,
in fact possible,to consider only a relative time which has no simultaneous global value, but which preserves the causal order of
events within the system.[19]

FOOTNOTES

1. A proposed "Frame Mode DTE" interface is an alternative to the X.25 interface.

2. Distributed algorithms for deadlock detection are given in [Mena 79]

3. Distributed algorithms for obtaining mutual exclusion have been discussed in [Lamp 74], [Dijk 74], and [Lela 77]. A different approach to mutual exclusion is the use of time stamps for regulating the access to distributed data bases (see for example [Thom 76] or

4. See for example [Zimm 75].

5. Based on this possibility, continuous renaming of ports is proposed in [Farb 75] for obtaining protection.

6. The distinction between names, addresses and routing is explained in [Shoc 78].

7. [Wulf 74] elaborates on this distinction.

8. [Lind 76] gives a survey on the use of extended types, small protection domains, and capability based addressing to support security and reliable software.

9. This is a reason for building distributed operating systems as described in [Prob 77].

10. The use of encryption for authentication is discussed in [Need 78]

11. Protection issues in public data networks are discussed in [Clip 76].

12. A "Data Encryption Standard" has been defined by the
    US National Bureau of Standards.

13. Usually the keys are exchanged manually. Automated procedures
    for obtaining matching keys are considered in [Need 78].

14. Error recovery is related to fault-tolerance. For a review
    on fault-tolerant computing see [Aviz 77].

15. See for example [Mart 70], section 5. The HDLC standard
    [HDLC a] has adopted a particular cyclic code, adding 16 bits
    to each block of data.

16. See for example [Rand 75]. A review of these principles is
    also given in [Hech 76].

17. For a more detailed discussion, see [Wirt 77].

18. See for example [Lamp 78].

19. The concept of such a relative time is discussed in
    [Lamp 78] and [Boch 77 d].

CHAPTER IV

A GENERAL FORMALISM FOR THE DESCRIPTION OF SYSTEMS

This chapter presents a general formalism for the description of systems with parallelism[1]. The basic notions of parallel systems are defined in terms of this general model. The different system description methods, discussed in the following chapter, are presented as special cases of this model. These chapters make abstraction of any physical fragmentation of the system into several components. For the majority of this chapter the notion of parallel processes is irrelevant, only quasi-parallel state transitions are considered.

4.1. *THE BASIC MODEL*

4.1.1. *Transition systems*

The system to be described is characterized by a (usually infinite) set of possible states Q. At any given time, the system is in a particular state $q \in Q$. The system may effect a transition. We write $q \longrightarrow q'$ to indicate that the system may make a transition from state q to state q', and say that q' is "directly accessible" from q. A transition is considered instantaneous and atomic (however see section 4.1.3). Being in a state q, the system may select, after some finite time, any transition that is possible from q, for execution. Generally this freedom introduces non-determinism into the system behavior.

Definition : A system is "deterministic" iff for each $q \in Q$, there is at most one q' such that $q \longrightarrow q'$. Otherwise the system is "non-deterministic".

An example of a non-deterministic system is shown in figure 4.1.

4.1.2. Operations

There is a set O of operation symbols. A transition q ⟶ q' may be labelled with an operation symbol o∈O , which is written q $\xrightarrow{o}$ q' . The unlabelled transitions of the system may be written as q $\xrightarrow{\lambda}$ q' .

Definition : An operation o∈O is "enabled" in state q∈Q iff there is a state q' such that q $\xrightarrow{o}$ p' .

Definition : An operation is "functional" iff for each q∈Q there exists <u>at most one</u> q' such that q $\xrightarrow{o}$ q' . For a functional operation o∈O , the following entities are defined :

- The "enabling predicate" P_o : Q ⟶ *boolean* is a boolean predicate on the states of the system, which indicates whether the operation is enabled in a given state or not.

- The "transition function" F_o : Q ⟶ Q is a partial function on Q which is defined for those states where P_o is *true* (the operation is enabled) and indicates the new state of the system.

An example of a non-deterministic system with two functional operations is shown in figure 4.2.

4.1.3. Transitions and relations between states

The set of all transitions of the system can be considered a relation on Q×Q , which we write ⟶ . Clearly, any pair (q,q') is an element of this relation, (q,q')∈ ⟶ , iff q ⟶ q' . Similarly, each operation o∈O is associated with a relation, written $\xrightarrow{o}$ or simply o , which is defined by

$$(q,q') \in \xrightarrow{o} \text{ iff } q \xrightarrow{o} q' .$$

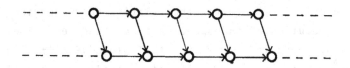

FIGURE 4.1

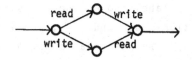

```
procedure outin;
    cobegin
        write (output,Y);
        read  (input, X);
    coend;
```

FIGURE 4.2

FIGURE 4.3

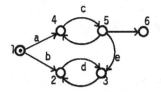

FIGURE 4.4

We write $o_1 \cdot o_2$ for the relation corresponding to the sequential execution of the operations o_1 and o_2, i.e. $q \xrightarrow{o_1 \cdot o_2} q'$ iff there is a q'' such that $(q,q'') \in \xrightarrow{o_1}$ and $(q'',q') \in \xrightarrow{o_2}$, i.e. $q \xrightarrow{o_1} q'' \xrightarrow{o_2} q'$. Similarly, we write $o_1 \cdot o_2 \ldots o_n$ for the relation corresponding to the sequential execution of n operations $o_1, \ldots, o_n$.

Figure 4.3 shows a particular labelling of the transition diagram of figure 4.1 with the operations o_1 and o_2, and indicates the pairs of the relation $o_1 \cdot o_2$. We note that a composite relation may be completely empty, although the components are not. An example is the following transition system :

$$Q = integer \times integer \ ;$$

the operations are o_1 and o_2, both functional :

$$P_{o_1} \equiv true \ ; \ F_{o_1}(x,y) = (0,y) \ ;$$
$$P_{o_2}(x,y) \equiv (x \neq 0) \ ; \ F_{o_2}(x,y) = (x, y \ div \ x) \ .$$

The relation $o_1 \cdot o_2$ is empty. A more familiar notation is the following : We consider a state space characterized by two integer variables X and Y, and two statements "X:=0" and "Y:=Y/X". Their sequential execution results in an undefined result (division by zero results in an exception condition). In the following sections, a notation such as

$$o_1 \ : \ x:=0 \ ,$$
$$o_2 \ : \ y:=y \ div \ x$$

will sometimes be used.

In the presence of unlabelled transitions in the system, it is sometimes useful to consider the relations generated by operations preceded or followed by unlabelled transitions. We call these relations generalized operations, and write $\hat{o}$ for the relation corresponding to the execution of an operation $o \in O$ preceded and followed by zero, one or more unlabelled transitions, i.e.

$$(q,q')\in \delta \quad \text{iff} \quad q \xrightarrow{o} q'$$

$$\text{or} \quad q \xrightarrow{o} q_1 \xrightarrow{\lambda} \ldots \xrightarrow{\lambda} q'$$

$$\text{or} \quad q \xrightarrow{\lambda} \ldots \xrightarrow{\lambda} q_1 \xrightarrow{o} q'$$

$$\text{or} \quad q \xrightarrow{\lambda} \ldots \xrightarrow{\lambda} q_1 \xrightarrow{o} q_2 \xrightarrow{\lambda} \ldots \xrightarrow{\lambda} q' \ .$$

4.1.4.   Abstraction

We consider the possibility that a system be described at different levels of abstraction, a higher description level showing less detail of the system's operations than a lower level. In the following, we discuss the relationship between two descriptions of a system at different levels of abstraction, within the framework of transition systems.

The lower level transition system, corresponding to a system description giving more detail, is characterized by a state space Q and a relation of transitions $\longrightarrow$ labelled by the operations $o\in O$. The higher level transition system, corresponding to an abstracted description of the same system, is characterized by a state space Q' , transitions, and operations $o'\in O'$. Q' corresponds to a partition of Q , such that each $q'\in Q'$ corresponds to a subset of Q within this partition. In general, not all subsets in the partition of Q are represented by a state $q'\in Q'$. Therefore the system, according to the detailed description, may be in a state for which there is no corresponding state in the abstracted description. This means that from the point of view of the latter, the system is in the process of making a transition (which is, however, considered an undivisible operation). In the particular case that each subset of Q , corresponding to a $q'\in Q'$, consists of a single element, the state space Q' of the abstracted system may be identified with a subset of the states of the detailed system, i.e. $Q'\subset Q$.

The transitions of the abstracted system description correspond to the transitions of the detailed description, such that there is a transition $q_1' \longrightarrow q_2'$ iff there are two states q_1 and q_2 corresponding to q_1' and q_2' , respectively, and a finite sequence of transitions $q_1 \longrightarrow \ldots \longrightarrow q_2$.

The labelling of transitions in the abstracted system description is related to the labelling of the detailed description according to the "implementations" of the operations $o' \varepsilon O'$. An implementation of an operation $o' \varepsilon O'$ is the specification of the relation corresponding to o' in terms of the operations and generalized operations of the detailed system description. An implementation may be of the form

$$\xrightarrow{o'} = \bigcup_{k} s^{(k)}$$

where the $s^{(k)}$ are operation sequences of the form $s = \tilde{o}_{i_1}.\tilde{o}_{i_2} \ldots \tilde{o}_{i_n}$ and $\tilde{o}_{i_j}$ is either o_{i_j} or $\hat{o}_{i_j}$.

For example, we may define the operation *outin* of figure 4.2 by

$$\xrightarrow{\text{outin}} = \text{read.write} \ \bigcup \ \text{write.read} .$$

Another example is the definition of the operation of exchanging the values of two variables x and y using a variable z for intermediate storage as

$$\xrightarrow{\text{exchange}} = o_1.o_2.o_3 \ \bigcup \ o_4.o_5.o_6$$

where $o_1 : z:=x$ and $o_4 : z:=y$

               $o_2 : x:=y$ $o_5 : y:=x$

               $o_3 : y:=z$ $o_6 : x:=z$.

4.1.5.   *Parallelism and functionality*[2]

Definition : Two operations o_1 and o_2 "commute" iff $o_1.o_2 = o_2.o_1$, i.e. the result of their execution is independent of the order of execution.

For example, the operations $(x:=x+1)$ and $(x:=x-2)$ commute with one another, but do not commute with the operation $(x:=x*2)$. If the state space of the system is characterized by the values of the variables, a sufficient condition for two operations o_1 and o_2 to commute is

$$R_{o_1} \cap R_{o_2} = R_{o_1} \cap D_{o_2} = D_{o_1} \cap R_{o_2} = \emptyset$$

where R_{o_i} is the range of operation o_i $(i=1,2)$, i.e. the subset of those variables the values of which may be changed by the operation, and D_{o_i} is the domain of the operation, i.e. the subset of variables on which the new values may depend.

In the framework of transition systems, the consideration of parallelism is a form of abstraction. We consider first sequential execution to make the point. As above, we consider two descriptions of a system, one at a more detailed and one at a more abstracted level. Clearly, the sequential execution of two operations o_1' and o_2' in the abstracted description is implemented in the detailed description as

$$o_1'.o_2' = \bigcup_{k,k'} s_1^{(k)}.s_2^{(k')}$$

where we have assumed that the individual operations are implemented as

$$o_1' = \bigcup_k s_1^{(k)} \text{ with the } s_1 \text{ of the form } \tilde{o}_{i_1}.\tilde{o}_{i_2}...\tilde{o}_{i_n} \text{ ,}$$

$$o_2' = \bigcup_{k'} s_2^{(k')} \text{ with the } s_2 \text{ of the form } \tilde{o}_{j_1}.\tilde{o}_{j_2}...\tilde{o}_{j_m} \text{ ;}$$

i.e. an execution sequence of $o_1'.o_2'$ is a possible execution sequence of o_1' followed by one of o_2' .

The parallel execution of two operations o_1^i and o_2^i, written $o_1^i \| o_2^i$, is defined by considering the detailed description of the operations. A possible detailed execution sequence of $o_1^i \| o_2^i$ is obtained by merging two possible sequences of o_1^i and o_2^i, respectively. More exactly, if $s_{\|}$, of the form $\tilde{o}_{\ell_1} . \tilde{o}_{\ell_2} \ldots \tilde{o}_{\ell_k}$, is a possible execution sequence of $o_1^i \| o_2^i$, then there exist sequences $\tilde{o}_{i_1} . \tilde{o}_{i_2} \ldots \tilde{o}_{i_n}$ and $\tilde{o}_{j_1} . \tilde{o}_{j_2} \ldots \tilde{o}_{j_m}$ of o_1^i and o_2^i, respectively, such that

- $\tilde{o}_{\ell_1}$ is either $\tilde{o}_{i_1}$ or $\tilde{o}_{j_1}$,

- $k = n+m$ and

- if $\tilde{o}_{i_1}$, $\tilde{o}_{i_2}, \ldots, \tilde{o}_{i_{n'}}$ and $\tilde{o}_{j_1}$, $\tilde{o}_{j_2}, \ldots, \tilde{o}_{j_{m'}}$ are elements of $\tilde{o}_{\ell_1} . \tilde{o}_{\ell_2} \ldots \tilde{o}_{\ell_k}$ ($n'+m'<k$), then $\tilde{o}_{\ell_{n'+m'+1}}$ is either $\tilde{o}_{i_{n'+1}}$ or $\tilde{o}_{j_{m'+1}}$.

The relation corresponding to $o_1^i \| o_2^i$ is the union over all such sequences.

An example is the operation *outin* of figure 4.2, which may be defined as *outin* = *read* $\|$ *write*.

If o_1^i and o_2^i are functional operations, their sequential execution clearly is functional. This is not generally the case for parallel execution. The possible sequences for parallel execution include, as a particular case, the sequential execution sequences $o_1^i . o_2^i$ and $o_2^i . o_1^i$. Therefore the parallel execution of (x:=x+1) and (x:=x*2), for example, leads to a non-functional operation. A more interesting example are the operations $o_1^i = o_1 . o_2 . o_3 . o_7$ and $o_2^i = o_4 . o_5 . o_6 . o_7$, where $o_7 : x:=0$ and $o_1, \ldots, o_6$ are as defined above. We have $o_1^i = o_2^i$, and $o_1^i . o_2^i = o_2^i . o_1^i = o_7$, all functional. However, $o_1^i \| o_2^i$ is not functional (consider for instance the possible execution sequence $o_1 . o_4 . o_2 . o_3 . o_7 . o_5 . o_6 . o_7$ which is not equivalent to o_7).

Lemma : A sufficient condition for $o_1^i \| o_2^i$ to be functional is that each operation used for the implementation of o_1^i commutes with each operation used for o_2^i .

4.2.   REACHABILITY AND EXECUTION SEQUENCES

In this section, we consider a system which is initially in a given state and then evolves according to the possible state transitions. We do not consider a particular sequence of transition, but instead consider all possible transition sequences. We discuss some concepts and properties of systems which are of interest for system validation and analysis.

4.2.1.   *Possible operation sequences*

Definition : The "transitive closure" of a relation R is written R^* and defined as follows :

(i) $(x,x) \in R^*$;

(ii) $(x,y) \in R^*$ and $(y,z) \in R$ implies $(x,z) \in R^*$;

(iii)   all pairs of R^* are obtained by a finite number of applications of (i) and (ii) .

Definition : A state q' is "reachable" from a state q iff $q \overset{*}{\longrightarrow} q'$.

Definition : A state q is "final" iff it belongs to the set of final states, i.e. $q \in Q_F \subset Q$, which is an (arbitrarily) chosen subset of Q . A final state is characterized by the fact that the system may stay in such a state forever, even if further transitions are possible. In a non-final state from which further transitions are possible, the system <u>must</u> execute a transition after a finite time period[3].

Definition : An "operation sequence for state q" is a finite (possibly empty) or infinite sequence of operations corresponding to a possible sequence of transitions starting in the state q$\in$Q . We write $\sum_q$ for the set of all such operation sequences.

Starting in an initial state q , there are three reasons for obtaining a finite operation sequence :

(1)   The corresponding transition sequence is finite and terminates in a final state.

(2)   The corresponding transition sequence is finite and terminates in a state which allows no further transition.

(3)   The corresponding transition sequence is infinite, but consists almost uniquely of unlabelled transitions, i.e. after an initial (finite) sequence of transitions, all following transitions are unlabelled.

A situation where the system arrives in a non-final state which allows no further transition is called a "deadlock".

Definitions : A state q$\in$Q is "active" iff there exists a state q' such that q $\longrightarrow$ q' . A system is "deadlock-free" iff all states accessible from the initial state are active.

For example, the system of figure 4.4 with $Q = \{1,2,3,4,5,6\}$, $0 = \{a,b,c,d,e\}$, no final state $(Q_F=\emptyset)$ and initial state 1 , allows operation sequences of the following forms :

$$a.c.c^* \quad , \quad a.c.c^*.e.d^\infty \quad , \quad a.c^\infty \quad , \text{ and } b.d^\infty \quad ,$$

where we write "*" and "∞" to indicate a finite (possibly empty) and infinite repetition[4], respectively. The system has a deadlock in state 6, which accounts for the finite operation sequences of the form $a.c.c^*$.

4.2.2. Liveness

For most systems it is important to make sure that it
never stops (absense of deadlocks) and that certain states or operations can always be reached or executed again. Considering only
the case of transitions, we call these transitions the "key transitions" of the system. Similar to the choice of the final states,
the choice of the key transitions depends on the system design and
purpose (and is arbitrary, otherwise).

Definition : An "operation o is live" in a state q ,
written $\text{live}_o(q)$, iff there exist $q',q'' \in Q$ such that $q \xrightarrow{*} q'$
and $q' \xrightarrow{o} q''$.

Definition : A "system is live" iff all key transitions
are live in all states accessible from the initial state of the
system.

Definition : A state q is a "home state" of the system
iff q is accessible from all states accessible from the initial
state.

Lemma : If a system has a home state q_H and all key
transitions are live in q_H , then the system is live.

Lemma : A system with a deadlock is not live.

Considering, for example, the system of figure 4.4, we
see that the states 2 and 3 are accessible from all states, except
the deadlock state 6. If we introduce an additional transition from
state 6 to state 1, then states 2 and 3 are home states. If d is
the only key transition, the system is live.

4.2.3.   Equivalence between systems

Based on a comparison of the operation sequences that
may be generated by different systems, we define the notion of
"operational equivalence" as follows[5].

Definition : A system S' "simulates" a system S iff
for each state $q \in Q$ of S , there exists a state $q' \in Q'$ of S'
such that the set $\sum'_{q'}$ of operation sequences of system S' is
equal to the set $\sum_q$ of system S .

Definition : Two systems S and S' are "operationally
equivalent" iff S' simulates S , and S simulates S' .

The operational equivalence between two systems depends
on the level of details that are considered. Two systems may be
equivalent when considered at a high level of abstraction, while
the equivalence disappears when more details are considered. Sometimes it is sufficient to make abstraction from certain operations
in order to obtain an equivalence between two systems. For example, the systems of figures 4.4 and 4.5 are equivalent when abstrac
tion is made from the operation c .

4.3.   SYNCHRONIZATION MECANISMS

In the last section, we have considered all possible operation sequences that may be generated by a system starting in
some initial state. In this section we consider decision algorithms
to determine whether, after a given sequence of transitions, a given operation may be executed or not. Such algorithms are necessary for the system implementation. They may also be taken as a system description, because they determine which labelled transitions
are possible in each state of the system. Since they are effective
and determine the order in which the operations of the systems may
be executed, we call such an algorithm a synchronization mecanism.

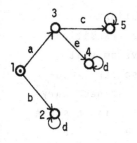

FIGURE 4.5

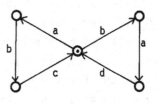

FIGURE 4.6

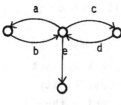

FIGURE 4.7

```
process p;
   begin O_1; O_2; ...; O_n end;
```

FIGURE 4.8

```
process p
   begin
      cycle O_1; O_2; ...; O_n end-cycle
   end;
```

FIGURE 4.9

We call "activation condition" of an operation o ,
written AC_o , a necessary condition for executing a transition
labelled o . It may be expressed in terms of the system state,
or in terms of the partial operation sequence σ_p so far executed by the system. For the example of figure 4.5, it is necessary
for the execution of the operation d that the system is in state
2 or 4, or equivalently that the executed partial operation sequence is of the form $b.d^*$ or $a.e.d^*$.

In the following, we use very often synchronization mecanisms of a particularly simple kind which are only based on execution counts for the different operations. A counter N_o is associated with each operation o , and counts the number of times a
transition labelled o is executed since system initialization ;
and an activation condition for a given operation may only depend
on the counters of (all) the operations. For example, the synchronization mecanism of the system of figure 4.5 is of this kind, but
the one for figure 4.6 is not of this kind, since the possibility
of executing the operation c depends on the order in which the
operations a and b were executed, and not only on the number
of times.

The semaphore is a popular synchronization tool[6]. A semaphore is an integer variable of special type on which only two
functional operations P and V exist. The P-operation on a semaphore sem is characterized by the enabling predicate
$P_{P(sem)} \equiv (sem > 0)$, and the transition function
$F_{P(sem)}(sem) = sem-1$. Similarly, the V-operation is characterized
by $P_{V(sem)} = true$ and $F_{V(sem)}(sem) = sem+1$.

Equivalently, a semaphore sem may be described by two
dummy operations P(sem) and V(sem) with activation conditions
depending on execution counters as follows :

$$AC_{P(sem)} \equiv N_{P(sem)} < N_{V(sem)} + K_{sem} \quad ,$$
$$AC_{V(sem)} \equiv true \quad ,$$

where K_{sem} is a constant (the initial value of the semaphore).

As additional examples for the specification of synchronization with execution counters, we consider a system with two operations a and b . If the activation conditions (considered as necessary and sufficient conditions) are

$$AC_a \equiv (N_a=0) \text{ v } (N_b=1)$$
$$AC_b \equiv (N_a=1)$$

the operation sequence of the system is a.b.a ; for the activation conditions

$$AC_a \equiv AC_b \equiv (N_b=0)$$

one obtains operation sequences of the form $a^*.b$. However, for obtaining operation sequences of the form $(a.b.c \cup b.a.d)^*$, it seems that counters are not sufficient for specifying the synchronization. However, activation conditions depending on the current system state (see for example figure 4.7) are clearly sufficient.

We note that in practice, several synchronization constraints are imposed on the operations of a system, each having a different origin. For example, a shared resource, the sharing processes, the system scheduling policy, etc., each may impose certain constraints on the order in which the operations of the system may be executed. Therefore the necessary and sufficient condition for the possibility of executing an operation is usually given by the conjunction of several necessary activation conditions. In the case of a functional operation o , one has

$$P_o \equiv AC_o^{(1)} \wedge AC_o^{(2)} \wedge \ldots \wedge AC_o^{(n)}$$

4.4. NON-INSTANTANEOUS OPERATIONS

Each transition of a system is considered an undivisible and instantaneous event. But for certain considerations, it is important to consider operations with a finite, non-negligeable execution time. Non-instantaneous operations may be described within the framework discussed so far, using an approach of abstraction as follows.

A non-instantaneous operation o' is considered at a more detailed level of description as the sequence $\overline{o}.o.\underline{o}$.(or simply $\overline{o}.\underline{o}$) of undivisible operations, where $\overline{o}$ is the beginning of the operation o' , $\underline{o}$ its end, and o is the operation proper (which may be of no interest for certain considerations). The sequential order of execution of the operations $\overline{o}$, o , and $\underline{o}$ implies the following activation conditions :

$$AC_o \equiv N_{\overline{o}} > N_o \quad ,$$
$$AC_{\underline{o}} \equiv N_o > N_{\underline{o}} \quad (\text{or} \quad N_{\overline{o}} > N_{\underline{o}} \quad , \text{respectively}) \; .$$

Definition : For a non-instantaneous operation o' , the "activity count", written $active(o')$, is equal to $(N_{\overline{o}} - N_{\underline{o}})$, and represents the number of operations o' in progress.

Lemma : The activity count of a non-instantaneous operation is always equal or greater than zero.

4.4.1. Mutual exclusion

Definition : Two non-instantaneous operations o'_1 and o'_2 are "mutually exclusive" iff the execution of one excludes, at the same time, the execution of the other, i.e. the predicate

$$active(o'_1) = 0 \quad \vee \quad active(o'_2) = 0$$

is always true.

Definition : A non-instantaneous operation o' is a "critical section" iff its activity count is never larger than one, i.e.

$$active(o') \leqslant 1 .$$

It is easy to see that the activation conditions

$$AC_{\overline{o}_1} \equiv active(o_2') = 0 ,$$

$$AC_{\overline{o}_2} \equiv active(o_1') = 0$$

impose mutual exclusion on the operations o_1' and o_2' , and that the activation condition

$$AC_{\overline{o}} \equiv active(o') = 0$$

make o' a critical section.

An example for mutual exclusion is the readers-writers problem[7]. A simple version of the problem is presented by a memory resource which supports *read* and *write* operations to be executed by different processes. In order to keep the data in the memory logically consistant, it is necessary that at most one *write* operation is executed at any given time (the *write* operation is a critical section), and in order to read consistant data the *read* operations must be mutually excluded from the *write* operations. Therefore the synchronization problem is solved by the following activation conditions[8] :

$$AC\,\frac{^{(1)}}{read} \equiv active(write) = 0$$

$$AC\,\frac{^{(1)}}{write} \equiv (active(read)=0) \wedge (active(write)=0) .$$

4.4.2. *Queuing considerations and scheduling*

In the above solution of the readers-writers problem, a large number of readers may prevent a writer from executing a *write* operation. In order to give priority to the writers, an additional activation condition may be established for the *read* operation which prevents reading when a writer is waiting. In this section, we consider this and similar problems which are related to queuing, priorities and scheduling.

A simple approach for including the aspect of queuing for the execution of a non-instantaneous operation, is to consider an additional step, i.e. the request step, in the sequence of primitive operations that make up the execution of the non-instantaneous operation. Explicitely, the execution of a non-instantaneous operation o' is described in more detail by the sequence $\dot{o}.\bar{o}.o.\underline{o}$, where $\dot{o}$ is the request of the operation o' , with the additional activation condition (to account for the sequential execution order)

$$AC_{\bar{o}} \equiv N_{\dot{o}} > N_{\bar{o}} \quad .$$

Now we can define the "waiting count" for an operation o' , written *waiting(o')* , as

$$waiting(o') = N_{\dot{o}} - N_{\bar{o}} \quad .$$

The usefulness of this approach for the description of synchronization problems is demonstrated by the following examples. For its implementation, it is sufficient to keep two counters for each operation, one for *active* and one for *waiting*[9].

The readers-writers problems with priority for the writers is solved by adding to the system description the following activation condition which expresses the absolute priority of the writers over the readers :

$$AC_{\overline{read}}^{(2)} \equiv waiting(write) = 0 \quad .$$

This is an example of several synchronization constraints being imposed for different reasons. $AC \frac{(1)}{read}$ is imposed for the logical consistancy of the system, and $AC \frac{(2)}{read}$ is imposed for priority considerations. The fact that these different aspect remain separate in the system description is an advantage of the method of using activation conditions for the specification of synchronization.

For giving equal chances, for accessing the resource, to readers and writers it seems to be necessary to have them wait on the same condition. This may be arranged by introducing a common primitive operation *enter* which is executed before the non-instantaneous *read* and *write* operations. If we adopt

$$AC_{enter} \equiv active(write) = waiting(write) = 0$$

as condition for "entering" the resource, *active(write)* = 0 is automatically satisfied at the beginning of *read* or *write* operations ; therefore this condition may be eliminated from the activation conditions $AC \frac{(1)}{read}$ and $AC \frac{(1)}{write}$.

4.5.   PROCESSES

As the discussions of the preceding sections show, many important concepts of parallel systems may be described by the model of transition systems without using the concept of processes We show in this section how this concept may be introduced into transition systems.

4.5.1.   The concept

In addition to the set of states Q , the transitions,
and the set of operation symbols O , we introduce a set P of
distinct processes p∈P . A transition of the system may not only
be labelled by an operation symbol o∈O , but also by one or more
processes p∈P which are those processes involved in the transition. Usually only one process is involved in a given transition;
transitions involving several processes realize some kind of inter-
process communication. For example, a *read* operation of the readers
writers system would involve (i) the resource (considered a process) and (ii) the "process" on behalf of which the reading is
performed.

Since each activation condition of an operation in the
system is usually related to a particular process, we consider
sometimes independent sets of execution counters for each process.
They are distinguished by superscripts indicating the involved
process. Such a process specific execution counter for an operation is only incremented when a transition labelled with the particular operation <u>and</u> the particular process is executed. For example, the activation conditions for the readers-writers problem
considered above depend on the execution counters associated with
the resource, not on those associated with the processes that call
on the resource. The following examples often involve the following kinds of simple processes.

Definition : A "simple sequential process" p is a process executing one given (finite) sequence of operations
$o_1.o_2...o_n$, as shown in figure 4.8. It implies the activation
conditions

$$CA_{o_1}^{(p)} \equiv (N_{o_1}^{(p)}=0) \quad \text{and}$$

$$CA_{o_i}^{(p)} \equiv (N_{o_i}^{(p)} < N_{o_{i-1}}^{(p)}) \quad \text{for} \quad i=2,...,n \quad .$$

Definition : A "simple cyclic process" p is a process executing a given (finite) sequence of operations repeatedly, as shown in figure 4.9, giving rise to an operation sequence of the form $(o_1.o_2...o_n)^{\infty}$. It implies the activation conditions

$$CA_{o_1}^{(p)} \equiv (N_{o_1}^{(p)} = N_{o_n}^{(p)}) \quad \text{and}$$

$$CA_{o_i}^{(p)} \equiv (N_{o_i}^{(p)} < N_{o_{i-1}}^{(p)}) \quad \text{for} \quad i=2,...,n \quad .$$

4.5.2. *Cooperation*

We consider as an example the cooperation between a producer and a consumer process, as shown in figure 4.10. The producer process generates messages and sends them to the consumer process which, in turn, consumes them. We discuss in the following first a system with direct coupling between the two processes, and then a system where the processes communicate through a message queue.

If we consider the sending and receiving as one undivisible operation, which we call *transfer* (at a more detailed level of description the *send* and *receive* operations may be both implemented by the *transfer* operation) we obtain the following assignment of processes to the operations :

- *make* implies the process *producer*,
- *transfer* implies both processes *producer* and *consumer*, and
- *use* implies the process *consumer*.

The activation conditions are (conditions for simple cyclic processes, as explained above)

$$CA_{make}^{(producer)} \equiv N_{make} = N_{transfer}$$

$$CA_{transfer}^{(producer)} \equiv N_{transfer} < N_{make}$$

$$CA_{transfer}^{(consumer)} \equiv N_{transfer} = N_{use}$$

$$CA_{use}^{(consumer)} \equiv N_{use} < N_{transfer}$$

A simple analysis shows that these conditions imply a synchronization between the operations of the system which may be represented by the state transition diagram of figure 4.11.

We call this approach to the communication of the producer and consumer processes "direct coupling", since the processes communicate directly with one another through the execution of a common transition[10]. This implies close synchronization for the execution of this transition. Another possibility is to insert a *buffer* process between the *producer* and *consumer* processes[11]. In this case, there is direct coupling of the *buffer* process with the *producer* and the *consumer*, but the synchronization between the *producer* and *consumer* is weaker, depending on the buffer size.

A finite *buffer* process, operating as a finite queue of maximum length K , is characterized by the fact that it executes the operations *send* and *receive* in such an order that the activation conditions

$$AC_{receive}^{(buffer)} \equiv N_{receive} < N_{send} \quad and$$

$$AC_{send}^{(buffer)} \equiv N_{send} < N_{receive} + K$$

are satisfied.

In the case of a *producer* and *consumer* communicating through a *buffer*, we obtain the following assignment of processes to the operations :

- *make* implies the process *producer*,
- *send* implies the processes *producer* and *buffer*,
- *receive* implies the processes *consumer* and *buffer*, and
- *use* implies the process *consumer*.

```
process producer;
    var  m:  message;
    begin
        cycle make(m); send (m) cycle-end
    end;

process consumer;
    var m:  message ;
    begin
        cycle receive (m); use (m) cycle-end
    end;
```

FIGURE 4.10

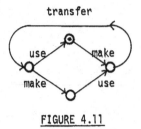

FIGURE 4.11

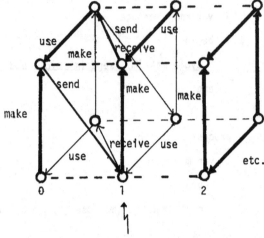

number of messages in buffer

FIGURE 4.12: Synchronization between a
producer and consumer obtained
by a buffer queue.

```
procedure use-resource;
    begin use; ...; use end;
process p_i;
    begin
        cycle work_i; use-resource cycle-end
    end;
```

FIGURE 4.13

```
critical section use_x;
critical section use_y;
process p_1;
    begin
        cycle x.use̅; y.use̅ ; ...; y.u̲s̲e̲; x.u̲s̲e̲  cycle-end
    end;
process p_2;
    begin
        cycle y.use̅; x.use̅ ; ...; x.u̲s̲e̲; y.u̲s̲e̲  cycle end
    end;
```

FIGURE 4.14: Two processes possibly leading to a deadlock

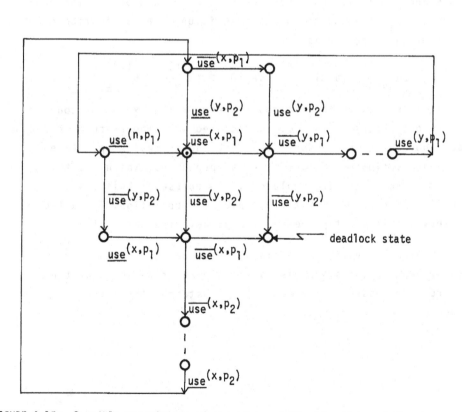

FIGURE 4.15: Possible transitions of the system defined by figure 4.14

The activation conditions of the *producer* and *consumer* are the same as above (replacing the operation *transfer* by *send* or *receive*, respectively). An analysis shows that these conditions and the activation conditions of the *buffer* imply a synchronization between the operations of the system which may be represented by the state transition diagram of figure 4.12.

4.5.3. *Mutual exclusion*

The discussion of mutual exclusion in section 4.4.1. remains valid when different processes are distinguished. We consider as an example[11] a resource process r with a critical section *use* shared by a number of processes p_i $(i=1,2,...,n)$ shown in figure 4.13. The process assignment to operations is as follows :

- work$_i$ implies the process p_i (for $i=1,2,...,n$) ,
- $\overline{use}$ and $\underline{use}$ imply the resource process r and one of the processes p_i (depending on the transition). The activation condition of the resource is

$$CA \frac{(r)}{\overline{use}} \equiv (active^{(r)}(use)=0) \equiv (N \frac{(r)}{\overline{use}} = N \frac{(r)}{\underline{use}}) \quad .$$

Here it is necessary to distinguish between the execution counters for the operations $\overline{use}$ and $\underline{use}$ associated with the resource process (used above) and those associated with the processes p_i (used in the activation conditions of these processes, which are the standard conditions for simple cyclic processes). This distinction is not necessary for the example of cooperation, where the counters of different processes always have the same values.

The activation conditions for mutual exclusion leave much freedom to the system as far as the relative speed of the different processes is concerned. For instance, the operation sequence

$$\overset{(p_1)}{\text{work}_1} \quad \overset{(p_2)}{.\text{work}_2} \quad \underset{}{\overset{(r,p_2)}{.\text{use}}} \quad \overset{(r,p_2)}{\underline{.\text{use}}} \quad \overset{(p_2)}{.\text{work}_2} \quad \underset{}{\overset{(r,p_2)}{.\text{use}}} \quad . \text{ etc.}$$

is allowed by the activation conditions, but usually not desirable
since process p_2 alone proceeds. Additional activation conditions
may be foreseen for obtaining the desired scheduling (see for example section 4.4.2).

Definition : A schedule is "fair" for a process p iff
it is excluded that the system does an unlimited number of transitions not implying process p where the system goes through an
unlimited number of states for which the activation conditions imposed by the process p alone would allow a transition that implies the process.

For example, the activation conditions for the readers-
writers problem given in section 4.4.1 seems to be unfair for a
writer process if the resource is flooded by readers. The
$AC \overset{(1)}{\overline{write}}$ may never become true because there is always some active reader. During all those reading transitions the activation
conditions of a writer process, waiting for the *write* transition,
will allow this transition. But the activation conditions are not
necessarily unfair. Activation conditions never force a transition, they only may prevent them. In this case, a scheduling algorithm is conceivable which lets *read* operations wait when a
process waits for writing (see for example section 4.4.2).

Systems with activation conditions for mutual exclusion
often lead to system deadlocks unless special precautions are
taken[13]. A typical example is given by two processes requesting
two critical regions in opposite order, as shown in figure 4.14.
If the processes p_1 and p_2 , each enter one critical region no
further transition is possible, as shown by the transition diagram
of figure 4.15. This deadlock is due to the interplay of the activation conditions of the critical regions for mutual exclusion
and the activation conditions of the processes p_1 and p_2 for

sequential execution[14]. The deadlock could be avoided by intelligent scheduling.

4.6. *THE INDUCTION PRINCIPLE*

Definition : A boolean predicate I on the states of the system is "invariant in respect to the initial state $q_0 \in Q$" , or shortly "q_0-invariant" iff

$$q_0 \overset{*}{\to} q \quad \text{implies} \quad I(q) \quad .$$

Definition : A boolean predicate I on the states of the system is "q_0-inductive" iff

$I(q_0)$ and

$[q \to q'$ and $I(q)]$ implies $I(q')$.

Proposition : A q_0-inductive predicate I is q_0-invariant.

A property of a system that is to remain valid during the entire operation of the system is naturally a q_0-invariant, where q_0 is the initial state of the system. Such a property is valid for the initial state and all reachable states of the system. The logical verification of a system may therefore be obtained by formulating the desired system properties in terms of state predicates and showing that these predicates are invariant in respect to the initial system state.

The "induction principle" expressed by the proposition above indicates that the invariance of a predicate may be proven by showing that the predicate holds initially and that it remains valid under all possible transitions. Usually, such a proof can be made considering separately each operation of the system[15].

As an example, we prove the lemma of section 4.4 stating that, for any operation o' of the system,

$$active(o') \equiv N_{\bar{o}} - N_{\underline{o}} \geqslant 0 \quad .$$

Clearly, this holds initially, since initially $N_{\bar{o}} = N_{\underline{o}} = 0$. Using the induction principle, we have to show that if *active(o')* ⩾0 holds before some transition is executed then it also holds after this transition. If this transition is labelled $\bar{o}$, it increments the execution count $N_{\bar{o}}$ by one ; *active(o')* ⩾0 will still hold. If the transition is labelled $\underline{o}$, it increments the execution count $N_{\underline{o}}$ by one; *active(o')* ⩾0 will still hold after this transition since the transition can only be executed when the activation condition $N_{\bar{o}} > N_{\underline{o}}$ holds. If the transition is labelled differently, the execution counts $N_{\bar{o}}$ and $N_{\underline{o}}$, and therefore the value of *active(o')* , are not affected.

4.7. DISTINCTION BETWEEN "CONTROL STRUCTURE" AND "INTERPRETATION"

Most of the above considerations about the relative synchronization of the different operations within a system are independent of the particular meaning of the operations. The part of the system which determines the order in which the different operations may be executed is sometimes called the "control structure of the system, when considered in contrast to the actual meaning of the operations, sometimes called their "interpretation" or "semantics". The reason for making such a distinction is that many system properties only depend on the control structure of the system, and are independent of the interpretation of the operations.

For example, the study of program schemas yields many interesting results on the structure and properties of programs, which hold for any possible interpretation or choice of the basic statements in the programs. Another example is the discussion of

mutual exclusion in section 4.4, where the actual meaning of the
operations for which the exclusion is enforced, is not considered
at all. Partial interpretation is introduced when the commutation
between operations is considered, as in section 4.1.5. Whether two
operations commute or not, clearly depends on their meaning.

The distinction between control and interpretation is
indicated in figure 4.16, which may also be viewed as an approach
to the implementation of a system. The control structure determines the order in which operations are to be executed by the interpretation part of the system. The latter usually contains the data on which the operations are performed. Usually, there is also
some feedback in the form of test values which is used by the
control structure to make certain decisions. For example, the control structure of the statement sequence

$$S_1 \; ; \; \underline{if} \; condition \; \underline{then} \; S_2 \; \underline{else} \; S_3 \; ;$$

may be represented by the diagram of figure 4.17. Here the value
of the *condition*, provided by the interpretation part, is used by
the control part for deciding between the operations S_2 and S_3 .

A given control structure for a system corresponds to a
certain set of possible operation sequences (as explained in section 4.2.1). If a particular interpretation is adopted for the
control structure the set of possible operation sequences is usually reduced, due to additional constraints introduced by the interpretation. For example, the above statement sequence with the interpretation

$$S_1 \; : \; x := 5$$

and

$$condition \equiv x > 0$$

yields only the operation sequence $S_1.S_2$, and not $S_1.S_3$ which
is, however, allowed by figure 4.17.

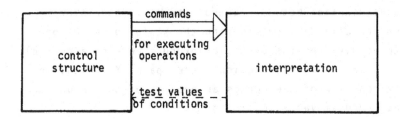

FIGURE 4.16: Distinction between "Control" and "Interpretation"

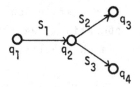

FIGURE 4.17

```
var i,x: integer;
    begin
      x := 1;  i := 1;
      while  i < n do begin  i := i + 1;  x := x * i  end
    end
```

FIGURE 4.18: Program for calculating N!

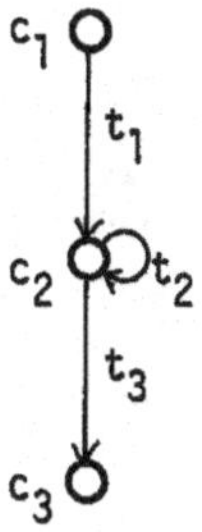

$P_{t_1} \equiv$ true $\qquad F_{t_1}(i,x) = (1,1)$

$P_{t_2}(i,x) \equiv i < n \qquad F_{t_2}(i,x) = (i+1,\ x*(i+1))$

$P_{t_3}(i,x) \equiv i \geq n \qquad F_{t_3}(i,x) = (i,x)$

FIGURE 4.19: Transition system equivalent to the program of figure 4.18

The distinction between control structure and interpretation may be formalized by considering the state space Q of the system to be given by the Cartesian product between a control state space C and an interpretation state space X (which, in turn, usually consists of the Cartesian product of the value spaces of several program variables); i.e.

$$Q = C \times X \quad .$$

4.7.1. Notation for the case of a finite control structure

For the case of a finite control state space of the form $C = \{c_1, c_2, \ldots, c_n\}$ and functional operations, we introduce the notion of a "controlled operation", which simplifies some of the following discussions.

Definition : A "controlled operation" t defined as a triplet (o, c_i, c_f) is the subset of those transitions of the operation o that go from a state (c_i, x) to a state (c_f, x') , where $c_i, c_f, \in C$ and $x, x' \in X$, i.e. a controlled operation is an operation restricted to given initial and final control states c_i and c_f , respectively.

While the enabling predicate $P_o(q)$ and the transition function $F_o(q)$ of an operation depend on the control part c and interpretation part x of the state $q = (c, x)$ of the system, the corresponding entities P_t and F_t for a controlled operation t can be expressed in a form only depending on the interpretation part x of the state space, since the control part is fixed, i.e.

$$P_t : X \longrightarrow boolean$$
$$F_t : X \longrightarrow X \quad .$$

For each pair of control states c_i and c_f , we define the set of possible controlled operations as

$$Tr(c_i,c_f) = \left\{ (o,c_i,c_f) \mid \text{there exist } x,x' \in X \text{ such that } (c_i,x) \xrightarrow{o} (c_f,x') \right\}$$

4.8.   ASSERTIONS

In the case of a finite control structure, and using the notation of section 4.7.1, we may write an arbitrary predicate on the state space Q in the form

$$I(c,x) = \bigwedge_{k=1}^{n} \left[c = c_k \quad \text{implies} \quad A_k(x) \right] ,$$

where the A_i are called "assertions". In order to show that I is (c_i,x_0)-inductive, it is sufficient to show that

$$A_i(x_0) \quad \text{and}$$

$$A_k(x) \wedge P_t(x) \wedge x'=F_t(x) \quad \text{implies} \quad A_{k'}(x')$$

holds for all k,k' and all $t \in Tr(c_k,c_{k'})$.

In the case of a sequential program, the induction principle turns out to justify the well-known method for program verification which associates assertions with certain places in the program text[16]. Each place in the program text corresponds to a control state $c_k \in C$, and a partial correctness proof of a program is equivalent to showing that the predicate

$$I(c,x) \equiv (c=c_f) \quad \text{implies} \quad A_f(x)$$

is (c_i,x_0)-invariant, where c_i and c_f are the initial and final control states, respectively, x_0 is the initial state of the interpretation part, and A_f is the assertion to hold when (and if) the program terminates. In practice, usually, a predicate stronger than I , saying somethings about the assertions at other places in the program, can be proven to be (c_i, x_0)-inductive, and therefore (c_i, x_0)-invariant.

As an example we consider the program of figure 4.18, which calculates n factorial, and which may be represented by the transition system of figure 4.19. We want to show that

$$(c=c_3) \quad \text{implies} \quad x=n! \quad .$$

This follows in fact from

$$(c=c_2) \quad \text{implies} \quad x=i! \quad \text{and}$$
$$(c=c_3) \quad \text{implies} \quad x=n!$$

which can be easily shown to be (c_1, i, x)-invariant for any integer i and x .

In the case of a shared resource with mutual exclusion for the operations of different processes on the resource, the induction principle turns out to justify the use of an invariant assertion $A_I(x)$ for specifying the consistancy constraints for internal variables x of the resource[17]. The control part of the resource may be represented by a single state c_0 , as shown in figure 4.20. Since there is only one control state, the (c_0, x_0)-invariance of A_I is proven by showing that

$$A_I(x_0) \quad \text{and}$$
$$A_I(x) \wedge P_0(x) \wedge x'=F_0(x) \quad \text{implies} \quad A_I(x')$$

for all possible operations o of the resource.

In the case of a control structure describing several parallel processes, a control state corresponds to a particular place in the program text of each process. Since each assertion is, in general, associated with a particular control state, the establishment of a correspondence between assertions and places in a program text is not possible like in the case of a sequentia' program[18].

.

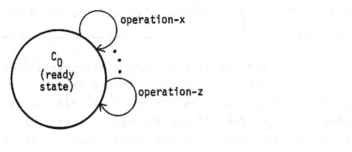

FIGURE 4.20

4.9.   FORMALIZED SPECIFICATION METHODS FOR SYSTEMS WITH PARALLELISM

The notions of state and state transitions, as explained in the sections above, seem to be the basis for most methods of system description. The different description methods that have been developed for different purposes seem to be specializations of the general formalism described above. Most description methods for systems with parallelism use either state transition diagrams or a programming language, in which case the execution of a single statement or a procedure may be identified as a transition. In certain methods, a process is a stable entity which is only rarely created or eliminated. In other methods, the degree of paralle-lism (i.e. the number of parallel processes) in a system varies continuously.

The operation of hardware, as well as software systems may be specified by Petri nets[19]. During the operation of a Petri net, the number of processes, represented by the tokens, usually varies continuously. In most cases, only "safe" Petri nets are considered, for which the number of tokens remains limited. Often it is possible to describe a system as a collection of several finite state automata which interact via input-output or other kinds of couplings[20]. Such descriptions may always be translated into the general context of Petri nets. To characterize the order in which certain operations may be executed, independently of the internal structure of a system, the method of path expres-sions has been proposed. Specifications based on path expressions may also be translated into Petri net implementations[21].

To add more descriptive power and flexibility, many extensions to Petri nets have been proposed. For example, the introduction of program variables leads to general models[22], which are related to "guarded commands"[23], whereas additional features may be useful for modelling computer and queuing systems, but lead to complex languages.[24]

Another approach to the description of systems with parallelism starts out from the concept of abstract data types or modules, as developed for the structured design of computer software. An abstract data module provides a certain set of interface operations which may be executed in interaction with the other modules of the system. Methods for specifying the interface operations without referring to the internal operation of the module are being developed[25]. This approach to specification may be adapted to systems with parallelism by considering, at a certain level of abstraction, the execution of an interface operation as an indivisible system transition.

Particular synchronization tools, to specify the order in which different operations may be executed in an environment of parallel processes, are conditional critical regions[26], monitors[27] and semaphores[28].

So far, we have ignored real time considerations. The state of the system determines which operations may be executed next, and it is assumed that one of the operations will be executed after some finite time. Therefore, no infinite loops may be involved in the execution of an operation. Real time considerations may be introduced in two steps (as explained in section 3.6) :

(a) Probabilistic real time constraints may be introduced by assigning a transition probability to each of the possible operations in a given system state, and by providing a probabilistic measure of the execution time of each operations. Such a Markov chain model may be used to derive response time and efficiency of communication protocols and interactive applications[29].

(b) Real time constraints are introduced by assigning minimal and maximal execution times for all operations[30]. This is the natural framework for describing time-outs (see section 3.6.1).

FOOTNOTES

1. The presented formalism is strongly influenced by Keller's general model of transition systems [Kell 76] and the approach to synchronization by Robert and Vergus [Robe 77]

2. A more detailed discussion of functionality in parallel system is given in [Coff 73], section 2.2.

3. The same distinction between final and non-final states is made in [Redz 77].

4. Infinite operation sequences of finite state systems are considered in more detail in [Redz 77].

5. This principle has been applied in [Pete 74] to the equivalence of different specification methods for parallel systems.

6. See for example [Dijk 68] or [Brin 73], section 3.4.

7. See for example [Cour 71] or [Brin 73], section 3.4.5.

8. This solution may be compared with the first solution in [Cour 71] using semaphores.

9. For more examples and detailed discussion see [Robe 77] and [Bekk 77].

10. Communication in the form of direct coupling is considered in [Boch 78] for finite state modelling of systems and in [Hoar 78] in the context of programming languages.

11. See for example [Brin 73], section 3.4.4.

12. See also [Brin 73], section 3.3.

13. For detailed discussion of deadlocks, see for example [Coff 73], section 2.3.

14. This view of deadlocks is taken in [Belp 75].

15. Several examples are given in [Kell 76].

16. See for example [Floy 67] or [Hoar 69].

17. See for example [Hoar 74].

18. The association of assertions with the elements of the product control state space of several processes is suggested in [Boch 77e]. The association of separate sets of (partial) assertions with the control states of the different processes, as suggested in [Ashc 75] is not of general applicability (see [Kell 67]).

19. An introduction to Petri nets may be found in [Pete 77].

20. See for example [Boch 77b] or [Boch 78].

21. See for example [Lane 75]. Path expressions are described in [Camp 74].

22. Such as [Kell 76].

23. [Dijk 75].

24. See for example [Noe 73]

25. See for example [Lisk 75], [Parn 77] or [Bart 77]. An introduction to the concept of abstract data types may be found in [Lisk 75].

26. See for example section 3.4 of [Brin 73] and [Kess 77].

27. See for example [Hoar 74]

28. [Dijk 68].

29. See for example [Masu 78] and [Whit 78]

30. A particular model for such real time systems is described in [Merl 76b].

CHAPTER V

ARCHITECTURE OF DISTRIBUTED SYSTEMS

Distributed systems are usually very complex. In addition to the system part which deals with the application proper, a large part of the system is concerned with the communication between the distributed components, exchanging data over great distances, and controlling the synchronization and consistency of the operations performed at different locations. This section deals in particular with this communications aspect of a distributed system.

Because of their great complexity, the design of distributed systems is usually structured into a certain number of hierarchical layers, as explained above (see section 2.3). Each layer provides some specific additional services (facilities), to be used by the next higher layer, and uses the services provided by the next lower layer. In using these services it ignores the details of their implementation in the lower layers. An example of such a layered system was first given for an operating system designed for a single computer and its peripherals[1] . In this case, the computer hardware is considered as being the lowest system layer, and the higher layers, implemented in software, each implement some particular facilities needed by the operating system and its users. The lower software layers are the following :

- Allocation of the physical processors to the different logical processes in the system : the facility provided by the layer is the (quasi-) parallelism of the different processes.

- Virtual memory management : the facility provided is a large virtual memory for each process.

- Dialogue with the operator : the layer provides, independently for each process, the possibility to converse with the operator.

- Input/output stream buffering : the layer provides the higher
  layers with a communications facility via logical input/output
  streams. (This facility is comparable to the communication
  transport service discussed below).

The communications part of a distributed system may also be structured into such a layered architecture, as explained in section
5.2. Sections 5.1 and 5.3 discuss particular aspects of the hierarchical system structure related to the physical distribution of the
functions. Section 5.4 deals with the problems of specifying, verifying and implementing the different layers and interfaces.

5.1.   LAYERED HIERARCHICAL SYSTEM STRUCTURE AND

PHYSICAL DISTRIBUTION

In this section we consider the communication between two
processes, but the discussion also applies to the communication
between more than two processes and may easily be generalized to
this case.

Figure 5.1 (a) shows two directly interacting processes.
We assume that, instead of directly interacting, two processes in
a distributed system communicate via some subsystem providing a
communication service, as shown in figure 5.1 (b). The communication subsystem is called "transparent" in as much as the direct
interaction between one process and the communication subsystem
appears, to the process, as a direct interaction with the other
process. Possible limitations to the transparency may be due to

(a)   throughput limitations,
(b)   delay,
(c)   limitations of the available interaction primitives,
(d)   transmission errors,
(e)   loss or duplication of messages,
(f)   loss of the message sequencing,
(g)   complicated interfaces to the communication subsystem, etc.

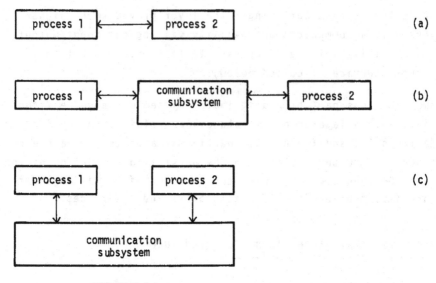

FIGURE 5.1

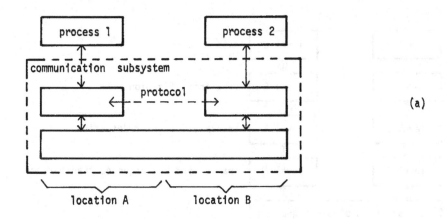

(a)

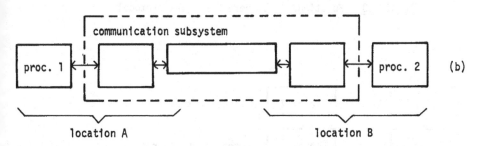

(b)

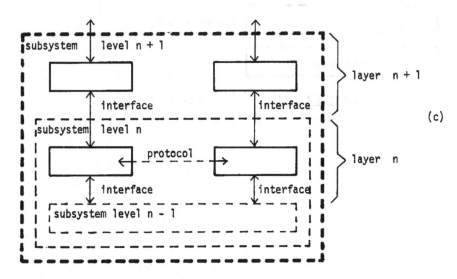

(c)

FIGURE 5.2: Layered structure of a communication subsystem

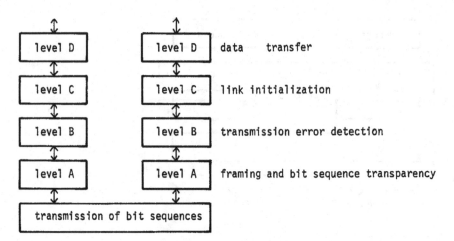

FIGURE 5.3: Functional sublayers of a link protocol

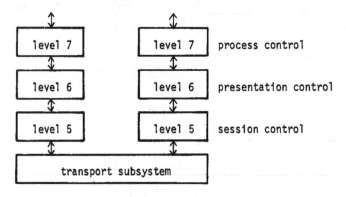

FIGURE 5.4: Higher level protocol layers

Figure 5.1 (c) is equivalent to figure 5.1 (b), but it is sometimes preferred because it shows that the communication subsystem provides a service which is used by the two processes, and that the two processes are considered as a higher layer within the hierarchical architecture of the system.

The communications subsystem itself is usually built as a hierarchical, layered system. Figures 5.2 (a) and (b) show an additional level of detail. Two system components, building the process-to-process communication service out of a more primitive communication service are shown, located with each of the communicating processes, respectively. They may be considered service processes which communicate with one another via the more primitive communication service, according to a particular protocol.

Figure 5.2 (c) shows a particular layer (of level n) within the hierarchical structure of the communication subsystem. The layer consists of two components providing the "level n" service to the next higher system layer. They follow the "level n" protocol for the communication between one another, and use the "level n-1" communication service provided by the next lower system layer. As examples of hierarchical communication systems, we may mention the protocol layers, for reliable communication over a dedicated physical circuit, and the protocol layers for Open Systems Interconnection, as shown in figures 5.3 and 5.4, respectively, and explained in section 5.2.

To show how such a layered communication subsystem may be used, we consider an application program that uses a data base. If the application and the data base are implemented in the same host computer the application program may be directly coupled to the data base access procedures, as shown in figure 5.5 (a). If the application program resides in a different computer a logically identical interface between the program and the access procedures may be realized by a communication subsystem containing several protocol layers, as shown in figure 5.5 (b).

The kind of communication service required depends on the characteristics of the interfaces between the distributed components of the application system, the interface between the application program and the data base access procedures in the above example. Sometimes the exchange of individual messages between different system components is an appropriate service, sometimes it is necessary to establish a certain number of logical links between system components, over which messages are sequentially delivered.

So far we have assumed that all the communication protocol layers are implemented together with the communicating application components. However, this is not necessarily so. As an example, figure 5.6. (a) shows a system where the protocols of figure 5.4 are partly implemented in a front-end computer and partly together with the application in the host computer. We note that the interface between the level 6 and level 7 layers goes through the connection between the front-end and host computers. However, the communication service provided by this (physical) connection may not be appropriate for this interface, in which case an additional protocol layer between the front-end and host computer may provide an appropriate interface, as indicated in figure 5.6 (b).

A similar situation arises when data transmission networks are used for communications. In general, certain services may have to be added by an end-to-end transport protocol layer to the service provided by the network, as shown in figure 5.7, in order to obtain the transport service desired. However, the network is usually implemented by switching nodes and transmission trunk lines, and the services can only be obtained through access lines over which particular network access protocols must be followed. Therefore, these network access protocols implement the interface between the network services and the end-to-end transport protocols, which are implemented in the subscriber equipment. This is shown in figure 5.8.

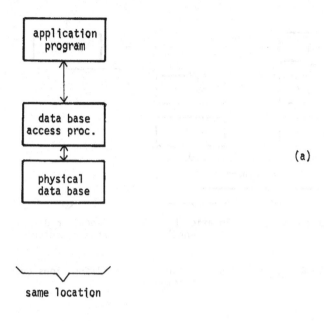

(a)

same location

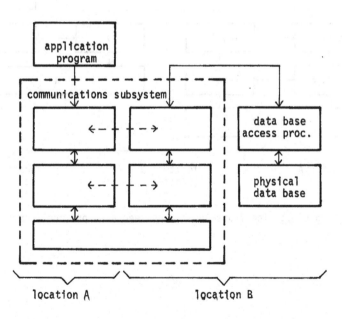

FIGURE 5.5: Local and distant communication with a data base

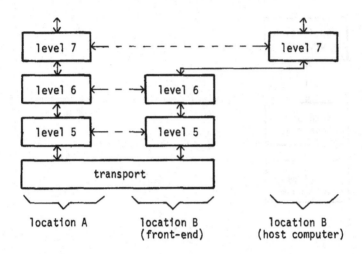

FIGURE 5.6(a): Distribution of protocol functions over front-end and host computer.

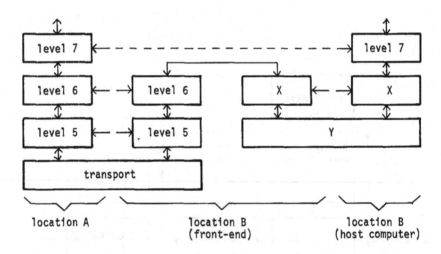

FIGURE 5.6(b): The front-end may be seen as a protocol converter

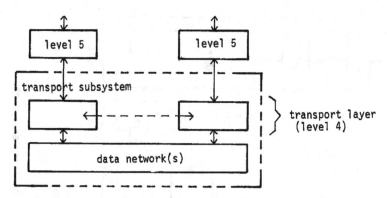

FIGURE 5.7: The transport sub-system

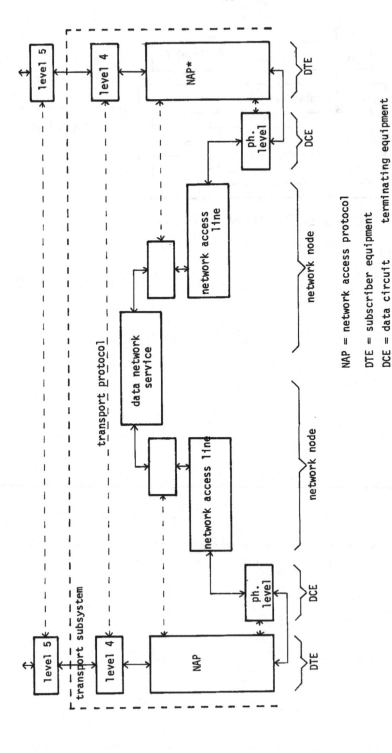

FIGURE 5.8(a): The transport subsystem:
Definition of "network access protocol" (NAP)

NAP = network access protocol

DTE = subscriber equipment

DCE = data circuit   terminating equipment

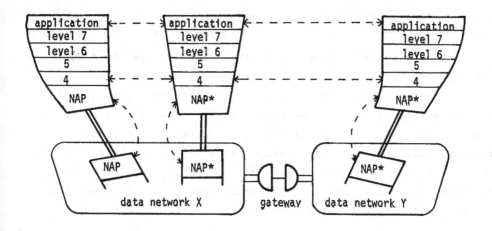

FIGURE 5.8(b): Protocols in a computer network
(NAP*: the NAP for different network
access lines need not necessarily be
the same)

5.2.   TYPICAL STRUCTURE OF A DISTRIBUTED SYSTEM

In comparing the communication functions implemented in different distributed computer systems, great similarity can be found between the problems handled in the different systems, although the methods of solving them may vary from one system to the other. Therefore, the idea of giving a typical structure of a distributed system consists of considering a layered architecture of the communication subsystem, as explained above, and indicating, for each layer, the problems handled by that layer. It seems that a similar structure applies to most distributed systems.

The interworking of different systems is clearly much simplified if their layered structure is the same and if, in addition, the same methods are used, in corresponding layers, for solving the same problems. Since interworking with other systems is an important requirement for most distributed systems, the development of standards in this area is of utmost importance[2] . National and international organizations are working on the elaboration of such standards, in particular the ISO (International Organization for Standardization) Subcommittees 6, on Data Communications, and 16, on Open System Interworking, of the Technical Committee TC 97 on Computers and Information Processing. The CCITT (International Telegraph and Telephone Consultative Committee of the International Telecommunications Union) defines standards for network access procedures for public data networks, which may also be used for private networks. Standard issues are also discussed in the Working Group 6.1, on Packet Switched Network Interworking, of IFIP (International Federation for Information Processing).

In the following subsections, we elaborate on the different layers of the typical structure of a distributed system. The structure of the lower layers, described in sections 5.2.1 and 5.2.2, are relatively well established. However, the higher level structure of distributed systems is still a subject for research and experiment, although the main characteristics, as described in sections 5.2.3 and 5.2.4, now seem to be generally accepted.

5.2.1. Communication over a dedicated circuit

A dedicated circuit is a means of transmitting data between two fixed locations. We describe here the problems handled in each of the layers, as shown in figure 5.3, within a subsystem which provides reliable data transmission between two fixed locations. More details are given in section 7. The ISO standard HDLC[3] also deals with these layers.

5.2.1.1. Transmission of bit sequences

We consider, as a basic communication service, the transmission of bit sequences in both directions, simultaneously or alternately, between the two locations. The service is characterized by

(a)   the nominal transmission speed (in bits per second),
(b)   the end-to-end delay,
(c)   the transmission error characteristics,
(d)   possible limitations of code transparency,
(e)   reliability and availability, etc.

Such a service is provided by analogue (for instance telephone) circuits with modems, and digital circuits. It is usually accessed through a standard interface protocol[4] , often called the physical interface, as indicated in figure 5.9.

5.2.1.2. Framing and bit sequence transparency

The service provided by this layer is the transmission of data blocks consisting of arbitrary bit sequences (i.e. there is bit sequence transparency), usually limited to a maximum length (typically 127 octets or longer). These data blocks are coded into "frames" which are sent over the basic communication service, and interspersed with "idle" traffic when no data is available for transmission. The service may be characterized by

(a)   fixed or variable data block length, and possibly a
      maximum data block length,

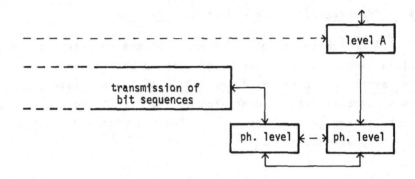

FIGURE 5.9: Physical level procedures are used to access a data transmission circuit

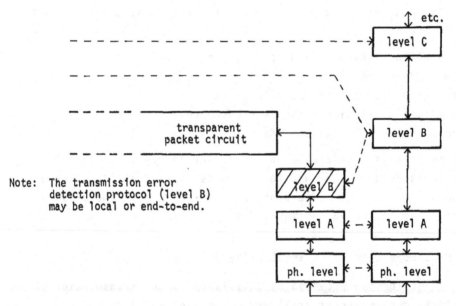

Note: The transmission error detection protocol (level B) may be local or end-to-end.

FIGURE 5.10: Local vs. end-to-end significance of link sub-layer procedures in the case of a transparent packet circuit.

(b) the probability of a transmitted data block being lost,

(c) the overhead introduced, etc.

in addition to the characteristics a, b, c, and e of section
5.2.1.1 above.

When provided on a commercial basis, such a service is
usually charged on the number of data blocks transmitted. It may be
accessed through an interface protocol containing two layers, as
shown in figure 5.10. We call such a service a "transparent packet
circuit"[5] .

We note that the asynchronous (i.e. start-stop) data transmission service may be considered a particular service with framing
and transparency, where the data blocks have a fixed length of one
octet.

5.2.1.3. Transmission error detection

The service provided by this layer is the transmission of
data blocks **and** the detection of possible transmission errors. Some
redundancy coding scheme is used to detect transmission errors. The
service may be characterized by

(a) the probability of undetected transmission errors,

(b) the introduced overhead,

and the characteristics of the lower system layers (see above).

5.2.1.4. Link initialization and reliable data transfer

The link initialization layer is concerned with establishing
agreement, between the communicating subsystems, on the status of
the communication subsystem, its initialization, and the recovery
from major faults of the layers below. The data transfer layer provides reliable data transmission by using retransmission techniques
to recover from (detected) transmission errors and loss of data
blocks. We note that these two aspects are not always as clearly

separated into distinct layers as indicated in figure 5.3.

In addition to reliable data transfer, the following facilities may be provided :

1. Flow control, i.e. the receiver may inform the sender of its readiness to receive more data (and the sender will wait for the receiver).

2. Fragmentation, i.e. the transmission of long messages as a sequence of packets which are transmitted in individual data blocks.

3. Out of band signalling, i.e. (high priority) transmission of short information not related to the normal data flow.

We note that the service provided by this layer, with the above facilities, corresponds to a (permanent) virtual circuit as provided by public packet-switched data networks according to CCITT Recommendation X.25.

5.2.2.   Communication through a network

Compared with a dedicated circuit, communication through a network is complicated by the fact that a given subsystem may exchange information not only with one, but with a large number of different subsystems located at different places. The different subsystems connected to a network, or several different interconnected networks, are usually distinguished by network subscriber addresses. The selection of the desired destination subsystem may be made in one of the following modes :

(a) long term selection : so-called "permanent" or "dedicated" circuits are established between subscriber addresses by the network administration

(b) medium term selection : real or virtual (packet-switched) circuits are established between subscriber addresses and cleared dynamically in accordance with an established network access protocol

(c) short term selection : the address of the destination sub-
     system is indicated in each data packet sent through the net-
     work. The establishment of a (logical) connection between sub
     scriber equipments is not needed prior to data transfer. This
     selection mode is adopted for datagrams[6] .

Consequently, a network access protocol, as shown in
figure 5.8, contains, in addition to a physical interface layer,
a network access layer which handles the selection of the destination subsystem, and the exchange of status information between the
network and the subscriber equipment. This layer also requires a
lower layer for framing and possibly transparency. In the case of
packet-switched virtual circuits, the remaining layers of figure
5.3 are also required, for accessing the transmission service provided by these circuits.

Present standards for network access protocols deal with
medium and long term selection : CCITT Recommendations X.21 and
X.25 deal with circuit switching and packet-switched virtual circuits, respectively. An alignment of these Recommendations into a
single set of protocol layers suitable for accessing circuit as
well as packet switched services, is a goal which should be attai-
ned with the definition of a common interface.[7] More details on
network services and access protocols are given in section
6.2.

5.2.3. *A uniform transport service*

While data networks and dedicated lines provide data
transmission between several physically distributed devices, such
as terminals, data bases, host computers, etc., the transport service provides the facilities needed for communication between
(logical) processes, such as application programs, terminals, host
computer log-in processes, data base access procedures, etc. The
communicating system components are identified not only by the
network subscriber address, but also by a so-called port. A host

computer operating system typically provides a large number of ports, some of them "well known" to the user community, through which the processes in the host communicate with one another and with external processes and terminals, as indicated on figure 5.11.

The communication facilities provided by the transport service may include

(1) process addressing, via ports,

(2) establishment and clearing of port-to-port associations,

(3) transport of "messages" (i.e. the logical units of the process communications) and short "interrupts", directly between ports or through established associations,

(4) protection against transmission errors,

(5) sequencing of messages (this includes protection against message loss and duplication),

(6) flow control of messages,

(7) delivery confirmation, etc.

We note that not all of these facilities are necessarily needed by all applications.

The transport protocol layer should be designed such that
(a) it may be implemented in many different environments in order to allow for the interworking of different computer systems, and
(b) the same transport service can be provided using different network transmission services, such as dedicated or switched circuits, packet switched circuits, or datagrams.

As shown in figure 5.8 (a), the transport protocol is an "end-to-end" protocol. For example, a facility such as delivery confirmation can only be implemented when the protocol operates end-to-end between the communicating processes. This is in contrast to network access protocols which have a local significance between the subscriber equipment and the closest network node. Certain kinds of end-to-end significance provided by a network transmission service may be lost in the case of transmission through several interconnected networks. More details on the transport layer are given in sections 6.1 and 6.3.

The message-oriented communication in a distributed environment has a noticeable impact on the design of computer operating systems. For a straight-forward interworking in a distributed environment, the operating system should be message oriented[8], and the inter-process communication facilities provided within the operating system should also be available from a distance[9]. Such a design also allows the different functions of an operating system to be distributed over several micro-computers coupled over a local bus, and other computer systems at larger distances[10].

5.2.4. *Higher level protocols*

The term "higher level protocols" usually means the end-to-end layers of a distributed system. In particular,it includes the transport layer described above and some additional layers, as shown in figure 5.4. The boundary between the layers of the communication subsystem and the distributed application layers is not exactly defined. Usually, the term "higher level protocols" denotes those layers of a distributed system (from the transport layer up) which provide functions that are sufficiently general to be used by a variety of different applications. Typical examples of higher-level protocols are the following :

(a) Terminal access protocols specify the interaction between an application program and a terminal, or between two terminals. To simplify the adaptation of application programs to different types of terminals and of terminals to different kinds of computer and operating systems, standard terminal access protocols have been proposed, also called "virtual terminal" protocols. Different classes of terminal access protocols may be distinguished depending on the functions they provide. We mention, in particular, access protocols for

- line-and/or page-oriented interactive character terminals[11],
- data entry terminals, handling forms which are structured into fields of characters,
- graphics terminals,
- batch terminals for remote job entry.

(b) File transfer protocols specify how complete data files may be transfered from one computer system to another[12]. Such a function may be used for remote entry of batch processing jobs, and for many distributed processing applications, including local edition of files.

(c) File access protocols specify how an application program may selectively access certain elements of a file at a different location. More elaborated forms of such protocols are used for access to data bases, as for example the highest layer of the communication subsystem of figure 5.5 (b). Different classes of file access protocols may be distinguished, such as:

- file transfer, i.e. obtaining a complete copy of a distant file (see above),

- record oriented file access, i.e. selective access (read, write or update) to individual logical records of a file, in random or sequential order,

- structure oriented file access, i.e. retrieval and update access to structured data bases.

The identification, selection, protection, etc., of the distantly accessed file is an additional problem which closely relates to the conventions of the operating system in which the file resides

The above protocols are also called "function-oriented" protocols, since each of them provides a particular set of functions used for obtaining access, from a distance, to a given kind of resource, such as terminals, files, data bases, etc. Many function-oriented protocols have been implemented in different distributed systems, often closely interwoven with the message transport mecanisms. They are different from one another, and interworking between these different systems is very difficult. New, standard function-oriented protocols are being proposed which could serve as the language for function-oriented interworking and be local-ly adapted to the different existing systems. In the development of such standards the following aspects are important :

(a) ease of adaptation to existing systems, and

(b) flexibility and open-endedness for future developments.

An agreement on standards for higher level protocols is essential for the interworking of different computer systems and for open system interconnection. The ISO committee on Open System Interworking (TC 97/SC 16) has established a "Reference Model" for the layered architecture of distributed computer systems in view of defining higher level protocol standards. This model contains the following layers[13] (as shown in figure 5.4) :

(a) Transport end-to-end control (as discussed in section 5.2.3).

(b) Session control : This layer is concerned with supporting structured dialogues ("sessions") between processes, such as, for example, an alternate mode of message exchange[14]. It may also contain functions for checkpointing and recovery from message transmission errors, as well as from errors and faults of the communicating processes[15].

(c) Presentation control : This layer is concerned with the repre-sentation and coding of data.

(d) Process control : This layer is concerned with the assignment, access and release of system resources, process initiation and termination and the establishment and termination of communica-tion sessions. It is closely related to the applications.

We note that the function-oriented protocols described above usually extend over several of these architectural layers. For example, a terminal access protocol includes conventions for dialogue control (session control layer), character coding (pre-sentation control layer), and terminal reservation (process control layer). A function-oriented protocol may be considered as being implemented in the process handling the resource on the one end, and in the process using the resource on the other end. An

appropriate end-to-end transport service (see sections 5.2.3) is
used for the exchange of messages between these two processes.

5.3.   COMPATIBILITY AND INTERWORKING ISSUES

The possibilities for interworking between different,
present day computer systems are very poor. This is due to the
large number of different conventions used by the different systems to provide the previously discussed functions (see section
5.2). The following are some of the reasons that have contributed
to this development :

(a) Different systems have grown independently of one another
over long periods of time.

(b) Different systems have different communication requirements,
which leads to different choices during the system design.

(c) During the initial design of a system, interworking with
other systems is often not considered a requirement.

Reason (b) above shows that there are limits to compatibility and interworking. The advantages of a standard layered system structure, such as the one outlined in section 5.2, relate to
the following :

- Standard protocols for a given system layer may be defined
independently of the other layers.

- For each layer, different protocols may be defined corresponding
to different communication requirements.

- For a given system, the protocols of each layer may be chosen
independently of one another in accordance with the communications and interworking requirements.

5.3.1. Requirements for compatibility

We now consider a given communications layer, as shown in figure 5.2, and ask the question : What are the points on which the subsystems of the layer must agree in order to guarantee a meaningful communication ?

There must be agreement, between the two sides, on the communication service provided at the upper interface to the next higher layer. This must be so, since the service provided over these interfaces may be used to replace a single interface between two subsystems, as indicated by figures 5.5. However, it is not necessary that the form in which this service is provided at the interfaces be the same on both sides. An example are the interfaces between the layers 6 and 7 in figure 5.6 (b).

There must also be agreement on the communication service used by the given layer (and provided by the interface with the next lower layer), but not necessarily agreement on the form in which it is accessed. (Note that this interface is the upper interface for the next lower protocol layer).

Finally, there must be a certain agreement on the way in which the two subsystems of the layer operate. The rules for their interaction through the communication service provided by the next lower layer, are called the communication protocol of the given layer. Certain aspects of the protocol are essential for the compatibility between the two subsystems, such as the meaning, format and coding of information exchanged via the lower communication layer, and certain rules about the order in which certain operations are executed in each of the subsystems. On the other hand, there are other aspects of the operation of the subsystems, also part of the protocol, which are not essential to compatibility, i.e. they may be changed in one subsystem alone without affecting the correctness of the given layer. However, these aspects have often an impact on the efficiency of the protocol. They may therefore be ajusted inde-

pendently in each subsystem such that the best operating conditions
be obtained.

5.3.2. *Network interconnection*

To allow for the interconnection of different circuits
and networks and the communication between subscriber equipments
connected to these different facilities, the communication service
provided by these facilities is usually such that the concatenation
of two or more such services, as shown in figure 5.12, results in a
logically identical service, the differences being of a qualitati-
ve nature, such as delay, maximal throughput, transmission error
characteristics, etc.

Therefore the data network service box in figure 5.8 (a)
may, in fact, be realized by the interconnection of several networks, each providing the same service. In practice, the interconnection between two networks must be realized through some
physical circuit over which appropriate access protocols must be
used. Such an interconnection is called a "gateway", and its architecture may be represented as in figure 5.13. The interconnection
is particularly simple in the case of dedicated physical circuits,
and datagram networks, respectively, because of the simplicity of
the services provided.

So far we have considered the interconnection of logically
identical transmission services. Interworking between transmission
services of different type is also possible. A simple way of interworking consists of adding a protocol layer on top of one of the
services such that it looks like the service it is to be connected
with. As an example, we consider the interworking between packet-
switched virtual circuits, real circuits, and transparent packet
circuits. Figure 5.14 shows the architecture of a system consisting of two networks, providing virtual circuits and transparent
packet circuits respectively, which are connected through a real
circuit. Subscriber equipments are also shown, connected to a net-

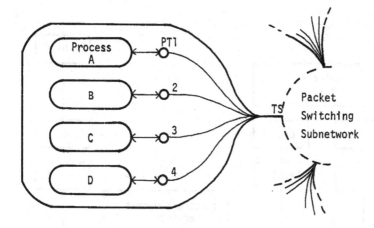

FIGURE 5.11: The concept of ports

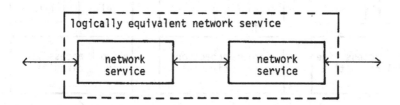

FIGURE 5.12: Concatenation of transmission services

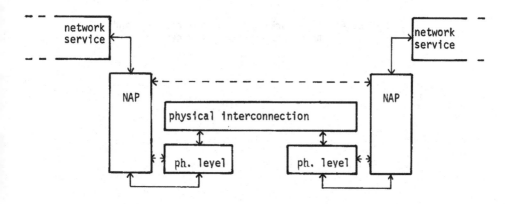

FIGURE 5.13: The structure of a gateway

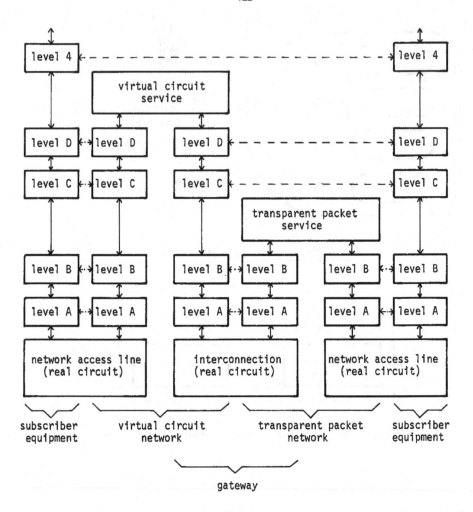

FIGURE 5.14: Interworking of virtual circuits and transparent packet services.

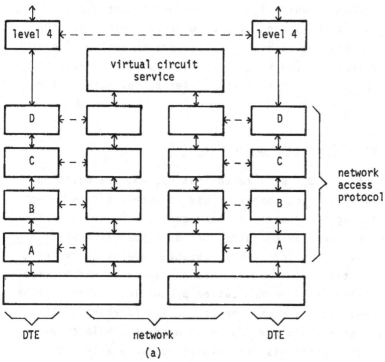

(a)

FIGURE 5.15: Communication through virtual circuits and transparent packet circuits using the same protocols.

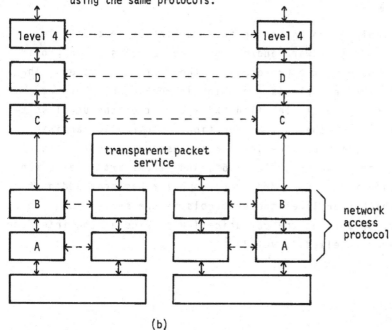

(b)

work through a real circuit, i.e. the network access line. This example, together with figure 5.15, also demonstrates that the same protocol layers implemented in a subscriber equipment may be used for interworking through networks with different services, as well as for separately accessing the different services of the networks [16] .

5.3.3. *System interworking and adaptation*

In section 5.3.1 we assumed that systems are built for interworking, and that the compatibility requirements are taken into account during the design. In many cases, however, this is not true. Most present day computer hardware and software, as well as terminals, are incompatible. Computer operating systems, as well as sophisticated terminals incorporate parts which corres- pond to several layers of communication protocols, although often not clearly identified as such. For direct interworking of the systems, these parts would have to be changed and replaced by mutually compatible protocols. Unfortunately, such a change is practically impossible because of the interwoven interfaces found in most systems.

A viable approach to the interworking of incompatible systems is to add (hardware and/or software) modules which provide an adaptation between the protocols of the different systems. The architecture of an example is shown in figure 5.6 (b) where we assume that the protocols labelled "X" are part of the usual soft- ware and hardware of the host at location B. To realize an inter- working with a system at location A which uses different protocol layers (labelled "level 5", "level 6", and "transport") for essen- tially the same function, a front-end computer has been added at location B which translates the protocols of one system into those of the other, preserving the communication service at the interface below the layer labelled "level 7" [17] .

As explained above, figure 5.6 (b) shows an example of
the adaptation of higher level protocols. We note that for the
interworking to be possible, there must be some compatibility at
some higher level (at level 7, in the example), i.e. there must be
agreement on what one system is going to do for the other. If this
is the case the lower protocol layers may be translated. We note,
however, that the end-to-end significance of the message exchanges
may be lost. In figure 5.6 (b), the transport, level 5, and level
6 protocols operate between location A and the front-end at location B, but not the host computer ; end-to-end significance would
remain at level 7 only if the box labelled "Y" included a data
transmission network.

5.4.   SPECIFICATION, VERIFICATION AND IMPLEMENTATION OF PROTOCOLS[18]

We explained in section 5.3.1 that the following points
must be agreed upon by the communicating subsystems, for each protocol layer :

(a) the service provided to the next higher layer,

(b) the communication service used, and provided by the next
    lower layer,

(c) certain aspects of the protocol operation (those aspects
    essential to compatibility).

It is therefore important to specify these points clearly and
precisely, as a basis for the design of the communication subsystem of a distributed system[19]. In addition, for the implementation
of each subsystem, the following points must be determined :

(d) the interface through which the service (point a above) is
    provided,

(e) the interface through which the communication service of the
    layer below (point b above) is accessed,

(f) the implementation of the protocol in the subsystem.

Clearly, these points must be consistent with the points a through

c above. The latter may be considered a more abstract description
of the former.

The verification of a protocol means to determine that the
interaction of the communicating subsystems according to the
protocol (point c above) using the communication service provided
by the next lower layer (point b above) does indeed result in the
service to be provided (point a above). Related to the implementation of a protocol, there is also the problem of verifying that a
given implementation in a subsystem (i.e. points d through f above)
corresponds indeed to the abstract specifications (points a through
c above).

5.4.1. *Specification techniques*

The broad meaning of the term specification is any information that helps describe the object being specified. However, its
proper usage in engineering is much narrower, involving the key
concept "abstraction". A specification should state all the requirements that an object must satisfy, AND NO MORE. To be abstract, it
must separate the essential from the inessential, covering the
former, and omitting the latter.

The question remains which techniques are best suited
for making specifications of services and protocols? Natural
language has the advantage of being easily understood, but usally
leads to lengthly and informal specifications which often contain
ambiguities and are difficult to check for completeness. Therefore formalized specification techniques have been developed to
aboid these disadvantages.

For the formalized specification of the services provided
by a given protocol layer (points a and b above), general proven
methods do not seem to exist[20]. A first step towards a complete
specification is certainly given by a list of the "service primitives" available at the inter-layer interface, with an exact decla-
ration of their parameters[21].

For the specification of the operation of protocols (point
c above), several methods have been used, which may be classified
as[22]

- transition diagram models,

- use of a programming language, and

- approaches combining transition models and a programming
  language.

Requirements for such specification methods include the description
of non-determinism and parallelism, and the support of abstraction
and stepwise refinement.

Formalized methods of protocol specification have been
found useful in many cases for the development of communications
standards and large scale data communication systems[23]. Formally
specified protocols are easier to check and verify than natural
language protocol descriptions. The implementation is facilitated
even if the formalized specification must be hand-translated
into a suitable implementation language[24]. Similarly, analytical
performance evaluation and the simulation of the protocols is facilitated. All this contributes to the validation and evaluation
of the system design and its implementation.

5.4.2. *Protocol verification*

The purpose of system validation is to assure that the
system satisfies the design specifications and (hopefully) operates to the satisfaction of its users. Validation activity is
important during all design phases; it includes the testing of the
final system implementation, simulation studies, analytical performance predications and verification. Verification is based on the
system specification and description, and involves logical reason-
ing. Therefore it may be used during the design phase before any
system implementation exists, in order to avoid possible design
errors. While testing and simulation only validate the system for
certain test situations, verification allows, in principle, the

consideration of all possible situations the system may encounter
during actual operation.

As mentioned above, the verification of the protocol of a
given layer may be defined as follows : To analyse the description
of the communicating subsystems of the layer and the service of
the layer below, in order to derive the communication service provided to the layer above, and to verify that it satisfies the
service specifications. This means to verify that the protocol
functions "correctly".

What can be verified? - As in the case of program verification, one may distinguish between (a) partial correctness
and (b) effective progress (also called "termination"). Since the
verification is based on the protocol and service definitions, an
important preliminary step is to check that the protocol description is complete, i.e. the behavior of each subsystem is defined
in all possible situations.

Partial protocol correctness means that, whenever a service
primitive is executed, it satisfies the local and global constraints
of the service specifications, but it does not imply that service
primitives will actually be executed. The verification of effective
progress proves that, in any possible situation, the next service
primitive(s) which may be executed according to the service specification will be executed within a finite delay after the layer
above has indicated its readiness for the primitive. In the case
of logical verification, which is the main focus of this section,
it is sufficient to assertain a finite time delay, which excludes
indefinite waiting. In the case that the efficiency and responsi-
veness of the protocol is to be verified, it is clearly nessessary
to determine numerically the expected time delay.

As far as effective progress is concerned, two kinds of
design flaws may be distinguished: deadlocks and "loops without
progress". A deadlock is a situation from which no further progress
is possible, and a partial deadlock is a situation from which the
execution of certain service primitives or sequences of primitives

is not possible any more. It is therefore essential to verify the absence of deadlocks and partial deadlocks (also called verification of "liveness").

A "loop without progress" is clearly undesirable since it may proceed forever, thus preventing any progress. It is distinguished from a dead-lock by the fact that the protocol will usually return to the normal mode of operation after a finite number of loop executions. However, infinite looping is not necessarily excluded. A common case of "loops without progress" are racing conditions, which last the longer the more the execution speeds of the involved entities are similar. (A typical example of racing is given by two parties that repeatedly try to telephone one another while they find the other's phone busy). For protocols involving contention, it is some-times hard to avoid the possibility of races. In such a case the number of repetitions of the loop may be limited by using different or randomly chosen execution speeds.

5.4.3. *Protocol implementation*

Protocol verification and implementation should be based on the same protocol specification and involve as few as possible transformations.[24] An example of a relatively straight-forward transformation of a formalized proto-col specification into an implementation in a high-level language is described in the Annex . We think that a suitable high-level language should support data structures, such as Pascal does, the concept of abstract data types, i.e. *class*, parallel processes, and the specification of the physical representation of data structures in memory. The use of such a high-level language simplifies the protocol implementation and its validation.[25] Without discussing the many different aspects that are relevant to protocol implementations we mention in the following only two particular aspects.

The incorporation of new communication protocols into an existing operating system is a very delicate problem. These problems must be solved for the host computers that participate in a heterogeneous computer network. In most cases, the user cannot count on must help from the computer manufacturers. Different solutions to the interworking of host operating systems with standard network protocols (network access, as well as higher level protocols) are des-cribed in the literature[26].

Using micro-processor technology, the different protocol layers of one local subsystem in a distributed system may be implemented on separate micro-processors with their own memory.[27]

FOOTNOTES

1. We refer to the THE operating system [Dijk 68b].

2. For a more detailed discussion of the compatibility issues involved, see section .3. The need for data communication standards is also pointed out in. [Sand 76] and [Boch 77c].

3. For an overview of HDLC [HDLC a, b and c] see, for example, [Sand 76], [Cott 77] or section 9.4.2.

4. A status report on these interface standards may be found in [Cott 77].

5. Switched and permanent transparent packet circuits are offered, for example, in Canada by the public Infoswitch data network.

6. A datagram service does not necessarily preserve the sequence of transmitted data packets, nor does it exclude the loss of data packets. See for example [Pouz 73].

7. See also section 6.3.2. For more details see, for example, G.V. Bochmann, "Frame Mode DTE interface", Report for the Department of Communications of Canada (1977).

8. Examples of such systems are described in [Brin 70], [Goos 72], and [Mill 77].

9. See [Akko 74].

10. See for example [Prob 77] and [Boch 79].

11. The role and nature of standards for access to character-oriented terminals is well described in [Barb 77].

12. The basic approach to file transfer is explained in [Gien 78]

13. This discussion is based on the ISO document TC97/SC16 N 117 (Nov. 1978).

14. A particular approach to this problem is based on the concept of a variable shared between the communicating processes [Hert 78].

15. A general approach to distributed error recovery is described in [Merl 77b].

16. Note that the figures do not show the protocol layer for network
    access. For more details see footnote 7.

17. The same principle is also applied to the interworking of different
    computer systems in heterogeneous computer networks (see for example
    [Davi 77]) and the adaptation of existing start-stop terminals to
    packet-switched data networks and Virtual Terminal protocols (see
    section 5.2.4).

18. The issues of this section are discussed in more detail in
    [Suns 79] and [Boch 79] .

19. The need for precise specifications is not particular to communication
    systems, it is encountered in any software development project (see
    for example [Parn 77]).

20. There are a number of methods proposed for the specification of
    software modules, in general, which would also be applicable to the
    specification of communication services, as for example described
    in [Lisk 75] , [Parn 77] , and [Bart 77] . A specific approach for
    specifying communication services is described in [Boch 80] .

21. For example, [Esch 78] contains such a specification for the service
    provided by a transport layer.

22. See [Boch 78b] for a review.

23. An experience with this approach has been described in [Boch 78c]
    see Annex.

24. The use of a formalized specification for verification and implementation
    is discussed in [Boch 75] for a simple example protocol.

25. Arguments are given in [Bels 78] and [Boch 79] .

26. See for example [Davi 77] or [Depa 76] .

27. Experiences with this approach are described in [Barb 77]
    and [Cave 78] .

CHAPTER VI

MESSAGE TRANSPORT REQUIREMENTS AND

DATA TRANSMISSION NETWORKS.

6.1.   *MESSAGE TRANSPORT REQUIREMENTS*

As explained in section 5.2, higher-level function oriented protocols rely on an appropriate process-to-process message transport service, which is provided at the interface of the transport subsystem. Depending on the applications, different communication requirements are encountered. These requirements may be characterized (i) by the way in which a communication partner is identified and selected, and (ii) by the following points :

(a) Message sequencing is provided over logical links, also called "liaisons", which may be established between two processes. Otherwise messages are sent independently of each other, and sequencing is not guaranteed.

(b) A maximum message length may be imposed by the transport subsystem.

(c) Throughput may be defined as the number of message-bits transported per second.

(d) Response time may be defined as the delay between the submission of a message by a process and the reception of the (complete) message by the destination process, provided the latter is waiting. Short response time for long messages requires a high transmission rate.

(e) Transmission error rates may be defined as the number of bit errors in received messages per number of received message bits. Two different rates must be considered :

- rate of <u>detected errors</u> concerning errors which are not recovered by the transport service but are detected and signalled to the transport users, and

- rate of <u>undetected errors</u>, concerning errors which are not signalled to the transport user (because they are not detected by the transport subsystem).

(f) The rate of <u>message loss</u> may be defined as the number of lost messages over the number of messages sent. Usually, losses are signalled to the transport user in the case of a liaison (but only in this case).

(g) <u>Reliability</u> may be defined as the expected period for which the specified transport service is provided without interruption.

(h) <u>Availability</u> may be defined as the percentage of time the specified service is available.

(i) <u>Security</u> is the assurance that the messages sent are delivered to the right destination, and are available only to this destination, and that only authorized processes may send messages.

In the following we give a list of some typical applications of distributed systems and their message transport requirements :

(1) Transaction systems for banking, sales control, etc. : The message transport requirements are characterized by fast response time, high throughput at the processing sites, and low undetected error rate. The maximum message length may be short (some hundred octets).

(2) Text editing : The requirements are as above, but in addition, text files must be transferred between the editing sites (in the future, terminals) and the document storage sites, which requires high transmission rates, low error rates and message loss, and long messages.

(3) Interactive graphics : As above; a high transmission rate is important.

(4) Remote submission of batch jobs : This application may be considered as a particular case of file transfer, characterized by high throughput, low error rates and message loss, and long messages.

(5) Distributed processing requires, in general, a mixture of long and short messages, good response time to shorten the time of resource utilization, and a low undetected error rate.

(6) Real-time control applications, in addition, usually need very good response-time characteristics for short messages.

6.2.   DATA TRANSMISSION SERVICES

Different data transmission services are provided by private and public networks and communication channels. They may be classified as follows :

6.2.1.   Dedicated circuits

A dedicated circuit provides a transmission path for bit sequences between two fixed points. It may be based on analogue or digital transmission techniques, such as telephone voice channels, broad band radio channels, possibly via satellites, digital circuits, or optical fibers. Except in the case of satellite links, the transmission delay is short (of the order of some milliseconds). The bit error rate of a circuit depends on the underlying transmission technology (order of 10^{-4} to 10^{-5} for telephone channels, 10^{-8} for digital circuits). Line protocols (see section 7) are usually implemented to adapt the transmission service to the communication requirements.

6.2.2. *Switching*

When a transmission network, or several interworking networks are used, the switching facility allows a user to dynamically
chose different communication partners. Except for possible (fixed)
multiplexing of several (logical) circuits over the same network
access path, the dedicated circuit connecting the user equipment
to the network (called "network access line") is either allocated
to one connection at a time, or shared between several connections
(statistically multiplexed). For dynamically established connections, the data transmission phase is preceded by a connection
establishment phase and followed by a clearing phase, which involve the exchange of the appropriate information between the user and
the network. In the cases of dedicated circuits, permanent packet-
switched circuits and datagrams, these additional phases are not
required.

6.2.3. *Circuit and packet switching*

Circuit switching provides, during the data transmission
phase, the equivalent of a dedicated circuit. The network access
line is dedicated to one connection at a time.

Packet switching networks provide the transmission of user
packets between the different user equipments. Packet switching is
characterized by a longer transmission delay (of the order of half
a second) and a low error rate. The following packet-switched trans
mission services may be distinguished :

- Datagrams : Packets are self-contained and travel independently
  of one another. No connection establishment and clearing phase
  is needed. Out-of-sequence delivery and packet loss is not excluded. There is flow control at the user-network interface.

- Virtual circuits (permanent or switched) : The data transfer
  phase of these connections allows for flow control, error reporting and interrupt transmission. Several connections may be

multiplexed through one network access line.

- Transparent packet circuits (permanent and switched) : The network access line is dedicated to one connection at a time, which during the data transfer phase, provides transparent transmission of packets from one end to the other.

The exact properties of the packet-switched services depend on the network providing the service. While the access protocol for virtual circuits to public data networks is internationally standardized (CCITT Recommendation X.25), there are certain variations in the service provided by different networks[1]. No standard exist, at present, for datagrams and transparent packet circuits.

Interworking between circuit and different packet-switched networks is possible if we assume that the purpose of the interworking is the provision of a message transport service with flow control, as defined in section 6.1, through the different networks. As shown in figures 5.14 and 5.16, it would even be possible that terminals or computers use the same protocol for obtaining the transport service, independently of the network to which they are connected. This requires, however, an agreement on such a standard protocol.[2]

6.3.   THE TRANSPORT PROTOCOL

As already mentioned in section 5.2.3, the role of the transport protocol layer is to provide the same message transport service, independently of the underlying transmission facilities used. In the case that a virtual-circuit transmission service is used, this service may be a sufficient transport service for certain applications therefore not requiring any additional transport protocol. For other applications the error performance, reliability or other parameters of the transmission service may not be sufficient, in which case on additional transport protocol would be used to provide the required service. An end-to-end transport protocol with an error detection and recovery function would also check the error performance of the underlying transmission service.

Figure 6.1 shows the system components that, together, provide the transport service. The local entity providing the service is usually called a "transport station". For each user, the transport station may select the most appropriate transmission service available and realize any additional end-to-end transport protocol in order to provide the required transport service.

Certain transport protocols are designed to operate over different kinds of transmission services, including datagrams, and interconnected transmission networks. These protocols are particularly robust, since they cannot rely on sequential packet delivery[3] Other transport protocols, more specialized, are designed for use over virtual circuits[4]. They provide additional error detection, reliability and end-to-end significance for message acknowledgements and flow control.

FOOTNOTES

1. The service provided by a particular network is well described in [Rybc 77].

2. The proposed "Frame Mode DTE" interface could be such a standard (see footnote 7 of section V).

3. See for example [Cerf 74] or [INWG 78]. [INWG 78] also contains a detailed description of the transport service provided.

4. See for example [Hert 78].

CHAPTER VII

LINE PROTOCOLS

This chapter deals with protocols used over a point-to-point physical communication channel. They provide a reliable data transmission service between the two stations connected via the channel, which is more or less unreliable. The different sections of this chapter deal with the different protocol layers into which a line protocol may be divided, as outlined in section 5.2.1.

Different kinds of data transmission services may be adopted for the communication between two stations, showing different characteristics such as the following :

(a) Transmission may be synchronous, asynchronous, or with flow control. In the synchronous case the transmission speed is fixed and usually determined by a clock; in the asynchronous case the speed is determined by the sender, though a maximum speed is imposed; whereas in the case of flow control the speed is determined by the sender and the receiver, within a maximum (the receiver indicates when he is ready to receive more data, and the sender indicates when new data is transmitted).

(b) The unit of transmission may be a bit, a block of bits of fixed size, or a block of varying size with a maximum size, or arbitrary long blocks. In the case of fixed size blocks, the information in a block may be presented to the receiver in parallel or sequentially, i.e. bit by bit. In the latter case, a clock is normally used to indicate when the next bit of a block is presented.

In this chapter we concentrate on protocols suitable for long distance communication, where the underlying physical channel provides bit sequential synchronous or asynchronous transmission[1]. The protocol layers discussed in this chapter build, on top of

this service, a quasi error-free, variable block size, data transmission service with flow control.

7.1.   TRANSMISSION OF BITS

The lowest level digital service is often called "physical level" and, for long distance communication, usually provides
bit sequential synchronous or asynchronous data transmission. The
essential characteristics of such a service are listed in section
5.2.1.

7.1.1.   Interface procedures

Different interface procedures (i.e. physical layer protocols, as shown in figure 5.9) may be used to access the bit
transmission service. The simplest interfaces are those for sequential bit transmission in asynchronous and synchronous mode.

A typical interface for asynchronous transmission is the
so-called "start-stop" interface[2] which consists of four interface
circuits, two (signal and return) in each direction of transmission
Separately for each direction, a continuous *one* signal means that
the sender is ready for data transmission. Data is usually transmitted in fixed-sized blocks of eight bits. To distinguish the
data from the continuous *one* signal, a so-called "start bit" of
value *zero* is inserted before each block; and to clearly identify
the start bit of an immediatly following block, a so-called "stop
bit" of value *one* is added after each block. If the next block
does not immediatly follow, the *one* signal of the stop bit is
extended up to the following start bit. A typical timing diagram
is shown in figure 7.1. To correctly receive the transmitted data,
the receiving station has to sample the received signal at appropriate times, as indicated in the figure. For this purpose it uses
a clock which runs at approximately the same speed as that of the
sender and is adjusted by every start bit.

A synchronous interface may be defined over the above interface circuits, but a typical interface standard[3] uses a common return for all signals, and provides two additional signal circuits for the exchange of control information between the transmission service and its user. The service provides bit timing signals, to be used for reception and sending of data, over an additional circuit. In this case the user equipment does not need a clock. Continuous synchronization between the timing signals at both ends of the connection is maintained by the transmission service (see also section 7.1.3).

7.1.2.   *Physical transmission media*

The simplest means of transmitting electrical signals is a pair of wires. A large number of parallel wires are used for local (parallel) interfaces, whereas simple twisted-pair wires are used over distances of up to several kilometers. The electro-magnetical properties of the installation impose a maximum useful speed (which may be measured in bits per second, or in frequency).

Optical fibers are a similar transmission means based on light, as opposed to electrical current. They are thin fibers of an optically transparent material which have the property of keeping the light, which enters at one end, within the fiber until it exits on the opposite end. Therefore they are also called "light guides". With the addition of suitable elements at the ends of the fiber for emitting and detecting the light, these fibers may be used for the transmission of electrical signals.

A different means are freely propagating electro-magnetic waves, such as radio or laser. Sometimes, radio waves are directionally focused, although less so than lasers, and are used to establish point-to-point connections which are functionally similar to the connections established by wires or optical fibers. Often, however, radio waves are broadcast, i.e. may be received at arbitrary places in a large geographical area. This is also true for transmission via satellite radio. The latter is charac-

terized by a transmission delay of about half a second, which is
several orders of magnitude larger than the delay through the
other transmission media mentioned.

In practice, the characteristics of a transmission medium
are strongly dependent on the equipment used to send and receive
the signals, and for the intermediate reamplification of the signal. Depending on the techniques used in these equipments, one
may distinguish between analogue and digital transmission channels[4].

An analogue channel transmits the continuous variations
of the input signal to the output side. Usually only variations
within a certain frequency range are transmitted. Typical examples
are telephone channels, and so-called "broadband" channels used
for television transmissions. For the transmission of digital signals over such channels, different modulation techniques may be
used to code the digital signals in terms of continuously varying
signals of certain frequencies[5]. For this purpose, modulation and
demodulation equipments (called modems) are placed at the sending
and receiving sides.

A digital channel distinguishes only two input or output
states, namely *zero* and *one*. This restriction simplifies the reception and reamplification of the signal, and leads to lower
transmission error rates. A digital channel may be used directly
for the transmission of digital signals. Usually a digital channel
is inherently either synchronous or asynchronous. With a suitable
coding technique, a digital channel may also be used to transmit
analogue signals. For example, pulse code modulation (PCM) is
used to transmit telephone conversations over digital circuits
in many telephone networks. In this case a synchronous channel
of 56 K bits per second is sufficient to transmit a voice frequency spectrum of up to 4 KHz. Inversely, the synchronous digital
speed that may be obtained over an analogue telephone channel
lies typically between 2400 and 9600 K bits per second, depending on the modems and channel quality[6].

7.1.3.   Bit synchronization

For the reception of a digital signal (or its reamplification, also called regeneration) it is necessary to know at which
instants the signal must be sampled to obtain the information trans
mitted. One possibility is to transmit the sampling information separately, for instance in the form of "new data signals" (in the
case of flow control), or in the form of the sender clock (in the
case of synchronous transmission). Over long distances, this approach, however, is not practical. Instead, the receiver usually
relies on its own clock which, of course, must run at the same
speed as the sender's clock. If it is not properly adjusted transmission errors occur in the form of inserted or lost bits, as shown
in figure 7.2.

In the case of synchronous transmission where the sender
and receiver clocks must stay synchronized over long periods of
time, the receiver cannot rely on a free-running clock alone, but
the receiver's clock is continuously adjusted to the sender's clock
by observing the transitions of the data signal. This adjustment is
only possible as long as sufficient changes occur in the data signal; long strings of either *zeroes* or *ones* may lead to clock desynchronization and cause transmission errors. Therefore this method leads to non-transparency (i.e. certain bit sequences are not
allowed as data) unless special precautions are taken (see section
7.2).

This synchronization introduces a kind of master-slave
relationship between the clocks of the sender and receiver. This
may lead to problems if additional synchronization constraints
are imposed on the clocks. For example, in the case of two-way
simultaneous (FDX) transmission as indicated in figure 7.3, the
sender and receiver at a given station usually use the same clock,
which leads to a circular timing dependence. In the case of a
synchronous network, as shown in figure 7.4, where the clocks of
all nodes must be synchronized, the problems of mutually dependent
synchronization relations are usually solved by introducing a

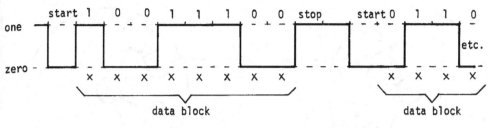

FIGURE 7.1: Timing diagram for asynchronous transmission

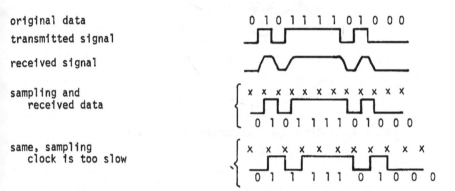

FIGURE 7.2: The importance of clock synchronization

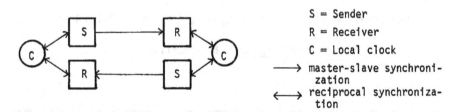

S = Sender

R = Receiver

C = Local clock

⟶ master-slave synchronization

⟷ reciprocal synchronization

FIGURE 7.3: Clock synchronization for two-way simultaneous transmission

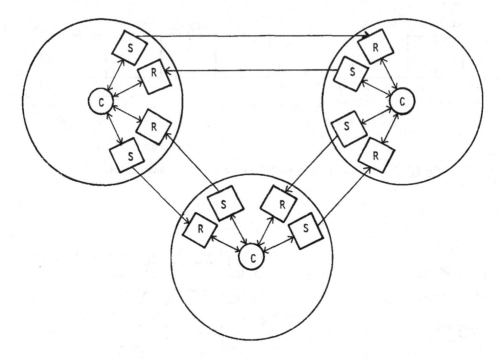

FIGURE 7.4: Clock synchronization in a network

data   0 1 0 1 1 1 1 1 1 0 0 0 1

bit stuffed data   0 1 0 1 1 1 1 1 0 1 1 0 0 0 1

transmitted signal   0 | 1 1 0 0 0 0 0 0 1 1 1 0 1 0 0

FIGURE 7.5: Bit-stuffing

data, coded for transparency

FIGURE 7.6: Character-oriented frame format

master clock on which all others depend either directly, or in
a linear chain. If the data processing related to the sender or
receiver is directly coupled (without intermediate buffering) to
the data transmission then the processing, too, must be synchronized to the transmission clock.

Most data processing applications, however, are not directly synchronized with the transmission speed. Instead, their
speed is synchronized through flow control which acts on information frames or packets, as explained below. Therefore the above-
mentioned synchronization problems do not exist in simple packet-
switched networks.

7.1.4.   Typical performances

The most important performance figures for bit sequentia
data transmission are the speed and the transmission error probability (see also section 7.3.1) of the channel. These figures are
shown in table 7.1 for some typical transmission channels.

Table 7.1 : Typical performance of data transmission channels

channel identification	typical speed (in K bps)	typical error rate
Low speed channels		
asynchronous, over telephone channel with modem	0.1 , 0.3	10^{-4}
Medium speed channels		
- asynchronous, over telephone channel with modem	2.4 , 4.8	10^{-4}
- synchronous, over telephone channel with modem	2.4 , 4.8	10^{-5}
- idem, conditioned channel	9.6	10^{-5}
- synchronous, digital	2.4 - 9.6	10^{-8}
High speed channels		
- synchronous, digital, for PCM telephony	56	10^{-8}
Very high speed channels		
- twisted pair wires, up to 100 m long		
- disk controller interface (byte parallel, asynchronous)		
- local bus interface (byte parallel, with flow control)		
- optical fiber		

7.2.   TRANSPARENCY AND FRAMING

As pointed out above, not all transmission services provide bit sequence transparency (i.e. all possible bit sequences may be transmitted); though this is an important requirement for data transmission. Also, the above mentioned services do not indicate where, within the continuous bit sequence of received information, a message starts. For most data transmission applications, it is important to know the block structure of the received data in order to be able to decode the received information. Therefore the data is usually structured into "frames" such that

the receiver is able to detect the beginning and end of each
frame. This also has the advantage that a transmission network
may distinguish between the reception of framed data and inter-
frame idle traffic.

The protocols providing transparency and framing, respectively, are usually closely related. In the following, we discuss
three typical methods.

7.2.1.   Bit-oriented method

The method described in the following is part of the ISO
standard HDLC[7], and is sometimes refered to as "bitstuffing".

Bit sequence transparency over physical channels that
do not transmit continuous sequences of *zero* or *one*, is obtained
in two steps. The first step is the bitstuffing, which avoids
continuous bit sequences of *one*. It provides the insertion of an
additional bit of value *zero* into the bit stream after each sequence of five consecutive *ones*. This additional bit is removed at the
receiving side. The second step, avoiding continuous sequences of
zero, applies the so-called NRZI coding to the resulting data
stream. This coding converts a *zero* bit into a change of state of
the transmitted signal, and a *one* bit into a "no-change". An example of the operation of this protocol is shown in figure 7.5.

So-called "flags" are used for framing. A flag is a bit
pattern of 0111 1110 in the bitstuffed data stream, which cannot
be obtained by bitstuffing, since it contains six consecutive *ones*.
Flags mark the beginning and end of a frame, and continuous flags
indicate idle traffic.

This bit-oriented protocol allows for frames of arbitrary length (in bits). It is usually implemented in specialized
hardware, since software implementations would be inefficient.

7.2.2. Character-oriented method

The method described in the following exists in a variety of different versions[8]. The basic idea is to reserve one escape character (i.e. *data link escape*, DLE) to indicate that the following character is not part of the data stream, but has a control function. For instance the beginning and end of a frame are indicated by the character sequences DLE STX *(start of text)* and DLE ETX *(end of text)* respectively. Transparency is obtained by inserting, from time to time, a DLE SYN *(synchronization)* sequence into the data stream, which ensures the necessary transitions of the transmitted signal; and a character of the data stream with the value DLE is transmitted as a DLE DLE sequence. The receiver has to perform the corresponding decoding.

The character-oriented method requires not only bit synchronization, as discussed in section 7.1.3, but also character synchronization, i.e. the receiver must know which received bit starts a new character. The character synchronization is obtained by preceding each frame by a sequence of at least two SYN characters; and when the receiver waits for a frame it looks for a SYN bit pattern. Note that the bit pattern of a SYN character is such that, within a sequence of several SYN characters, the only SYN bit pattern that may be found coincides with the original characters.

The complete frame format is shown in figure 7.6. We note that this format foresees two octets outside the data field for the error detecting code (see section 7.3). This means that the format is not cleanly spread between the transparency and framing layer and the error detection layer. The final PAD character is added because some receivers lose the last character of a received block.

7.2.3. Method based on envelope transmission

We now assume that the underlying physical transmission service provides transmission of envelopes, i.e. mini-blocks typically of eight bits each. Examples are a start-stop transmission service, or a synchronous service with an additional circuit which provides an envelope alignment signal indicating the beginning of an envelope, or the bits of an envelope may be transmitted in parallel. If transparency is not provided by the physical transmission service, it may be obtained by a scheme such as the character oriented method; or one bit in each envelope may be reserved to introduce an alternating bit value.

Although the physical transmission service delimits the envelopes, it is usually necessary to indicate which envelope begins and ends a frame. Again, either a character-oriented approach may be used, reserving certain envelope values for control functions, or one bit of each envelope may be reserved to indicate the presence of a "flag". We note that for the protocols above the framing level, the method of reserving a certain bit or field within a frame or message is the usual way to transmit control information. This is not possible without an underlying framing structure. In this context, envelopes may be considered as mini-frames.

7.3. TRANSMISSION ERROR DETECTION AND CORRECTION

7.3.1. Principles

The origin of errors

Transmission errors are introduced in most physical transmission channels by the statistical fluctuations of the received signal, or by "noise" introduced by switching or other external influences. Statistical fluctuations give rise to an error pattern where the probability, for a given bit of a transmitted sequence, to be erroneous is independent of the other bits in the sequence. This property is called "bit independence"; it implies that for a bit error probability of p , the probability for two consecutive bits to be both in error is of the order of p^2 , which is usually much smaller. On the contrary, externally introduced noise often gives rise to burst errors, which are strings of two to ten, or more, bits containing several bit errors. While single bit errors are relatively easy to detect and correct, this is much more difficult for burst errors (see below).

Typical error performances for certain transmission channels are shown in table 7.1. We note that telephone channels have a strong component of burst errors due to switching noise, while radio transmission channels usually exibit bit independent transmission errors.

Apart from the errors introduced by the physical trans- mission channel, errors may be introduced within the communication system layers above. For example, transmission errors may be intro- duced by a malfunction of the transparency and framing hardware discussed above, or by a central memory error in a switching com- puter.

Error detection and correction

For a given system layer, any of the following approaches may be taken in respect to transmission errors :

(a) Errors are ignored as far as possible. We note, however, that errors in the control information of the layer may lead to apparent protocol errors and desynchronization between the communicating partners.

(b) Errors are detected as far as possible, and reported to the next higher system layer. The higher layer will usually per- form an error recovery.

(c) Errors are detected and recovered as far as possible within the same layer.

For the approaches (b) and (c), the performance may be characte- rized by the overhead introduced on the one hand, and the proba- bility that an error is not detected (for (b)), and that an error

is either not recoverable, or not detected or wrongly recovered
or introduced by the recovery mecanism (for (c)), on the other
hand. In the case of error detection, the probability p that
an undetected transmission error occurs within a given data block
may be calculated as

$$p = \sum_i p_i \cdot q_i$$

where the sum is taken over all types of errors that may occur,
p_i is the probability of an error of type i in the block, and
q_i is the probability that an error of type i is not detected.

Error detecting or correcting codes are used for approaches (b) or (c) respectively. In both cases, redundancy is introduced into the transmitted data which allows the detection or correction of transmission errors by the receiver. Neither types of
code require any feedback from the receiver to the sender. However,
error detecting codes are usually used in conjunction with a next-
higher system layer which applies some kind of retransmission protocol to recover from the error; and this protocol relies on feed
back in the form of acknowledgements (see section 7.4.1)[9].

Architectural consideration

The layered structure of a typical communication system
architecture is explained in chapter 5. As pointed out, the recovery of transmission errors is typically performed by an error
detecting code and a retransmission protocol operating over a
dedicated or switched circuit. However, many variations exist.

If the error performance obtained by a standard system
structure, characterized by an effective error probability p ,
as given above, is not sufficient for an application, an additional error recovering system layer may be introduced. The resulting error probability p' is then given by

$$p' = \sum_i p_i \cdot q_i \cdot q_i'$$

where the q_i and q_i' are the probabilities that an error of
type i is not detected by the standard and additional layer respectively.

Error correcting codes may be used in situations where
retransmission protocols are inefficient, for example in the case
of high error probabilities, or long transmission delays, in particular over satellite channels. If introduced in an additional architectural layer below the framing layer, error correcting codes
will reduce the probability that frames are lost due to transmission
errors, and the number of errors detected in the layers above will
be smaller, thus reducing the frequency of retransmissions.

In the case of communication through a network (see for
example figure 1.3), many different transmission links are involved;
for instance network access lines, links between the network nodes,
and possibly front-end to host computer connections. In most cases,
transmission errors are recovered separately on each link, as shown
by the architecture of figure 7.7 (a). In the case of recovery by
retransmission, such step-by-step error recovery is more efficient
than end-to-end recovery as shown in figure 7.7 (b)[10]. However, in
the case of step-to-step recovery, the effective end-to-end error
probability is approximately

$$p = p^{(1)} + q^{(2)} + \ldots + p^{(n)}$$

where the $p^{(i)}$ are the effective error probabilities of the individual links with their respective error recovery mecanisms. It is
clear that the end-to-end error performance can never be better
than the worst link. In this case, an additional end-to-end error
recovery mecanism could be interesting. Usually incorporated in the
transport layer, it leads to a lower error probability p' , as mentioned above, and also detects (and possibly recovers) eventual mal-
functions in all the system layers below the transport layer.

7.3.2. Error detecting codes

Most error detecting codes used are block codes, which means that for each block of information a redundant error detecting code is calculated and sent together with the information. A typical frame format is shown in figure 7.8. The receiver calculates the code using the same algorithm, and if the calculated code is not the same as the received one a transmission error must have occured. The most important codes are the following :

(a) Simple parity : A parity bit is added to each information block. A transmission error is detected if and only if an uneven number of bits in the frame are in error. This is not sufficient for most applications.

(b) Longitudinal parity or checksum : In the case of an information block structured into bytes (i.e. octets or central memory words), as shown in figure 7.9, an additional byte is added containing the longitudinal parity (calculated byte-wise), or the higher-order truncated byte sum of the information block. For an arbitrarily erroneous frame, the probability of non-detection is 2^{-r} , where r is the number of bits in a byte. These error codes are particularly suited for software implementation.

(c) Cyclic codes : This is a large class of codes which are based on polynomial division modulo 2. Each cyclic code is characterized by a particular polynome P of order r , and coefficients 0 and 1 . The information block, in turn, is interpreted as a polynome and divided by P . The rest of the division is the code and contains r bits. As in the case above, the non-detection probability for arbitrary errors is 2^{-r} , but with a suitable choice of the polynome P it is possible to obtain codes which detect all errors involving two, or an uneven number of bits, or burst errors with a length smaller or equal to r.[11] A simple implementation of these codes in specialized hardware is possible.

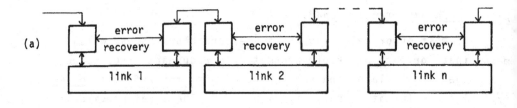

(a)

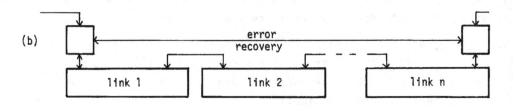

(b)

FIGURE 7.7: Step-by-step and end-to-end error recovery

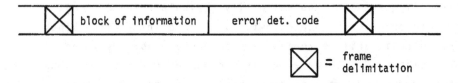

FIGURE 7.8: Typical frame format with error detecting code

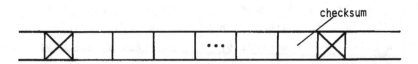

FIGURE 7.9: Frame format including checksum

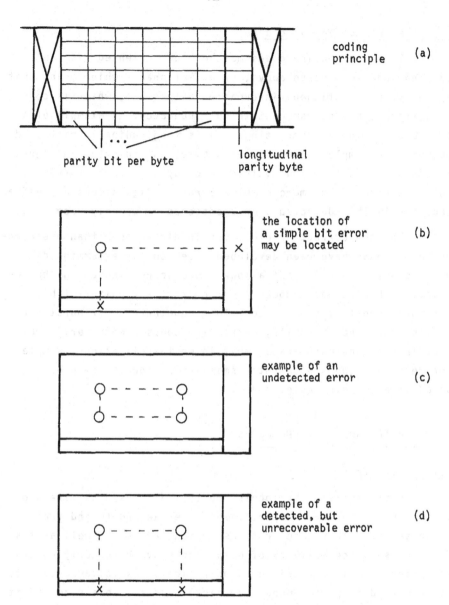

coding
principle   (a)

parity bit per byte   longitudinal
                           parity byte

the location of
a simple bit error   (b)
may be located

example of an
undetected error   (c)

example of a
detected, but   (d)
unrecoverable error

FIGURE 7.10: Error detection and recovery with parity

7.3.3.   Error correcting codes

Error correcting codes may be block oriented, as the
detecting codes discussed above, or evolutionary, which means that
they apply to a continuous information bit stream, which is coded
as a different bit stream containing redundancy. An example of a
simple block oriented correcting code is longitudinal parity used
together with simple parity for each byte, as indicated in figure
7.10. As shown in the figure, this code may be used to correct
single bit errors, but more complex error configurations are either
unrecoverable (but detected), or undetected or wrongly recovered.

For the correction of errors involving more than one erroneous bit, codes have been developed based on large Hamming distances between the different allowed code words, including the redundancy[12]. Evolutionary codes, too, correct any number of bit
errors provided they are not too close together[13]. For burst errors
involving more than two bits, correcting codes become very complicated. This is the main reason why, in most applications, simple
error detecting codes with retransmission protocols are used
instead of error correcting codes.

7.4.   RETRANSMISSION PROTOCOLS

7.4.1.   Principles

Retransmission protocols are typically used as line protocols or, as part of a transport layer, over an end-to-end transmission service. They recover transmission errors, as well as loss
and out-of-sequence delivery of data blocks by the underlying transmission service. The principle of operation is as follows. Data to
be transmitted is partitioned into packets of suitable size, if it
is not presented already in this form. The packets are sequentially
numbered by the sender and kept in a data buffer until their correct
reception at the other side is known to the sender. The packets are
transmitted sequentially, together with their number and a transmission error detecting code. The receiver checks the error code

and the sequence number to ensure that the packets are accepted in the right order and without errors. Via a feedback channel, the receiver returns acknowledgements, or sends retransmission requests to the sender if packets are missing or errors are detected. In the case of data transmission in both directions, this process is duplicated for each direction. Then the feedback information, for transmission, may be associated with the data packets transmitted in the opposite direction (this is called "piggy-backing").

The procedures described rely on an initialization procedure which establishes agreement, between the sender and receiver, on the sequence number of the first data packet to be transmitted. This procedure is also important for restarting data transmission after a failure. For example, a long term failure of the underlying transmission service leads to repeated packet loss or transmission errors. If a given data packet is retransmitted a certain number of times without success, the situation is usually considered a failure unrecoverable by the retransmission protocol. This is indicated to the next higher system layer, and may be followed by a reinitialization of the retransmission protocol.

Many different factors influence the efficiency of a retransmission protocol. The most important aspect is the maximum data throughput. In the case that data packets are handled one by one (i.e. protocol of type "alternating bit") the optimal packet size may be determined from the error probability and transmission overhead (size of framing, error detection and retransmission control information)[14]. In the case of several outstanding, i.e. non-acknowledged, packets and data transmission in both direction, the situation is quite complex[15]. The buffer size of the sender is also an important design consideration. It must be equal to the packet size times the maximum number of outstanding packets. This, in turn, is related to the transmission speed and the delay in obtaining acknowledgements[16]. We note that the number of outstanding packets is also limited by the number of bits reserved for representing the sequence numbers in the transmitted frames, because a cyclic numbering scheme is used. Another design consideration is the

choice between a sequential or selective retransmission strategy.
Selective retransmission means that the sender retransmits only
those packets for which the receiver detected loss or an error. A
simpler strategy, but less efficient when many packets may be outstanding, is sequential retransmission, which implies retransmission
of all packets starting from a lost or erroneous packet, and possibly retransmission of some packets that were already successfully
transmitted.

Usually, retransmission protocols also provide flow control,
i.e. producer-consumer synchronization, for the next-higher system
layer. The mechanisms used to provide flow control may be classified
as either stop-and-go or credit schemes. In the case of stop-and-go,
the sender may send a packet anytime, and may be told by the receiver
that it is "not ready", in which case the packet must be retransmitted
when the receiver is "ready". This is a very simple scheme, but generates unnecessary traffic. If the protocol operates over a dedicated
circuit this extra traffic is not harmful, since the circuit could
not be used for any other purpose anyhow. However, if the protocol
uses a shared transmission service, such as in the case of several
logical links being multiplexed over one circuit, or in the case of
end-to-end protocols, this extra traffic decreases the overall system efficiency. In these situations, a credit scheme is preferable,
since it generates no extra traffic. The sender may send a data
packet only after it has received the necessary credit from the receiver. The receiver would usually allocate the necessary buffer
space for the reception when it sends the credits to the sender[17].

The concept of a "window" may be used to describe the
packet sequencing and flow control mechanisms[18]. The window of the
sender includes the sequence numbers of the outstanding packets,
possibly to be retransmitted, and the numbers of additional packets
that may be sent according to the flow control rules. The window of
the receiver contains those sequence numbers which guarantee, when
received, that the accompanying data packet is an expected one and
not an outdated version. Both windows must be small enough as to
avoid sequencing ambiguities due to the cyclic numbering scheme.

A typical situation is shown in figure 7.11.

7.4.2.   The "alternating bit" protocol

We call the protocol described below the alternating bit
protocol because it uses a single bit to represent the sequence
number of a data packet. Although very simple, it shows a robust
behaviour in respect to errors of the underlying transmission service, and is one of the earliest protocols described in the literature[19]. It has been used in several networks, and many retransmission protocols in commercial operating systems operate in a simi
lar manner[20].

The protocol uses the underlying transmission service in
a two-way alternate mode, and provides reliable data transmission
simultaneously in both directions. Each communication station has
a *send buffer* containing the next data packet to be transmitted,
and a buffer to receive the next data packet from the opposite
station. It has in addition an *alternating bit* variable, which
indicates the sequence number of the next data packet to be sent.
The operation of a single station is shown in figure 7.12. Each
frame transmitted contains the alternating bit of the sending station and the contents of the *send buffer*, unless it is empty.

No initialization procedure is given for this protocol.
It is assumed that station A starts out in state 1, and the other
in state 3 with an empty send buffer, while the initial value of
the *alternating bit* variable is *one* in both cases. In the absence
of transmission errors, only the fat transitions of figure 7.12
will be executed. A transmission error, detected by some error detecting code in the system layer below, will lead to a retransmission of the last frames in both directions. The loss of a transmitted frame will lead to a deadlock, unless time-out transitions
are introduced, as indicated in the figure. It is assumed that
these transitions may only be activated in one of the stations,
and only after a certain time-out period has elapsed since the
transmission of the last frame.

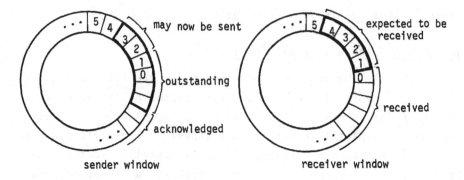

FIGURE 7.11: The "window" concept

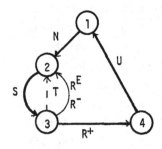

S = send frame

R⁺= receive frame with new data, i.e. received bit=alternat. bit for station A, ≠ for station B

Rᴱ= receive frame with detected error

T = time-out

N = new data into *send buffer*, and change alt. bit

U = use received data

FIGURE 7.12: Transition diagram for an alternating bit protocol station

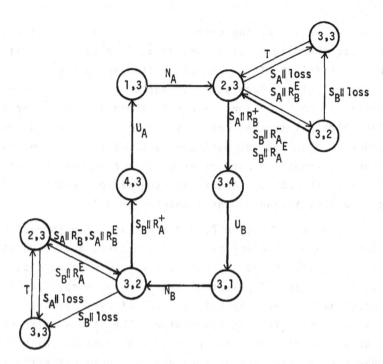

<u>FIGURE 7.13</u>: Overall system states reachable in the alternating bit protocol
(Notation: $S_A \| R_B^+$, for instance, means that station A does the
transition S, which is followed by the transition R^+
of station B).

	address field	control field	information field	error detecting code	
✕	address field	control field	information field	error detecting code	✕

```
1 octet                           2 octets
```

<u>FIGURE 7.14(a)</u>: HDLC frame format

	bits	0	1	2	3	4	5	6	7
information (I) frame			N(R)		P/F		N(S)		0
supervisory frame			N(R)		P/F	X	X	0	1
unnumbered frame		X	X	X	P/F	X	X	1	1

<u>FIGURE 7.14(b)</u>: Coding of the HDLC control field

An analysis[21] of the operation of two communicating stations leads to the diagram of figure 7.13. It shows the possible
states and transitions of the overall system which are reachable
from the initial state. Each state in the diagram is characterized
by the states of both stations, and only those states of the overall
system for which all transmitted frames have been received (or lost)
are considered. The time-out period is assumed to be chosen such
that a time-out transition occurs only after a message has actually
been lost, i.e. it must be longer than the maximum response time of
the other station, including the transmission delays.

The diagram of figure 7.13 demonstrates the correct operation of the protocol. One may see, by inspection, that each state
of the overall system has a successor, i.e. there is no deadlock,
and except in the case of permanent transmission errors or losses,
the operation always leads back to the normal cycle of operation,
which is indicated by the fat transitions. The diagram also shows
that the order in which the data packets are exchanged with the
next-higher system layer are always such that only correctly transmitted packets are delivered, and no duplication or losses may occur.

7.4.3. The HDLC classes of procedures

The alternating bit protocol, explained above, provides
adequate recovery from transmission errors and losses, but presents
several shortcomings. It cannot take advantage of a simultaneous
two-way transmission service; it is inefficient when the transmission
delay is longer than the time required to transmit a data packet;
and there are no proper reinitialization and flow control mechanisms.
The HDLC classes of procedures, for example, overcome these problems.
The following description is based on the HDLC standard[22], but the
same principles of operation may also be found in many other related
protocols designed for simultaneous two-way transmission and possible transmission delays.

Basic_properties

The following basic properties of the HDLC classes of procedures make them suitable for application in a variety of different situations. The standard specification concentrates on the protocol aspects which are essential for compatibility between different stations, and leaves unspecified many other aspects, which may be chosen for each protocol implementation according to the specific requirements.

In order to cater for a delay between the transmission of a data packet and its acknowledgement, HDLC uses cyclic (modulo 8) sequence numbering. Up to seven data packets may be transmitted without being acknowledged[23]. The acknowledgements are returned in the form of a *receive sequence number* NR which acknowledges all packets up to the number (NR-1). Acknowledging NR numbers may be piggy-backed in the information (I) frames, which transport a data packet in the opposite direction, and are also contained in supervisory frames which are used for retransmission and flow control. The format of the transmitted frames is shown in figure 7.14.

A cyclic error detecting code is included in each frame. A received frame with a detected error is ignored, which is equivalent to being lost. The loss of I frames is recovered as follows. The receiving station keeps a *receive variable* VR which always contains the sequence number of the next data packet to be received; and out-of-sequence received packets are not accepted. If a packet is lost the following packets will not be accepted, and therefore not be acknowledged. After a time-out period, the sending station will sequentially retransmit the packets that have not been acknowledged. As an option, the receiving station may also send a *reject* (REJ) supervisory frame as soon as the reception of an out-of-sequence packet indicates that the previous packet was lost. This accelerates the recovery process, since the sending station may start the retransmission as soon as the REJ is received.

A kind of stop-and-go flow control mechanism is provided by the supervisory frames *receive ready* (RR) and *receive not ready* (RNR), which may be sent by the receiving station.

The three different classes of HDLC procedures, described below, may be distinguished. They are not compatible with one another, but it is possible that a given station be capable of communicating according to several classes.

Unbalanced class with normal response mode (NRM)

This is the simplest HDLC class of procedure. It is called "unbalanced" because one of the communicating stations is considered to be "primary" and has the overall control of the communication link, while the other station is a "secondary" which only "responds" to the "commands" received from the primary.

In normal response mode, the secondary station may only send frames when it is polled by the primary. For this purpose, the primary sets the P-bit of a transmitted frame to *one* (see figure 7.14). When this P-bit is received by the secondary, it may transmit a sequence of frames, where the last frame of the sequence is indicated by a F-bit of value *one*. State diagrams controlling the normal response mode of the primary and secondary stations are shown in figure 7.15, and a typical sequence of exchanged frames is shown in figure 7.16, where it is assumed that the transmission service supports two-way simultaneous transmission, and data transfer takes place in both directions.

Unbalanced class with asynchronous response mode (ARM)

This class is similar to the one described above. However, in asynchronous response mode the secondary, as well as the primary, may send frames at any time.

In this response mode, the P/F-bit may be used by the primary station for "checkpointing", which is a mechanism by which the primary may recognize a particular received frame as being the

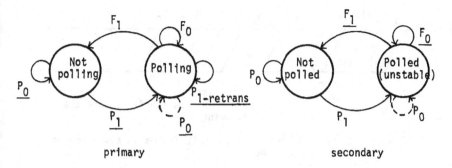

FIGURE 7.15: HDLC normal response mode (Note: Dotted transitions in full duplex transmission only.
An unstable state must make a sending transition at the earliest opportunity.

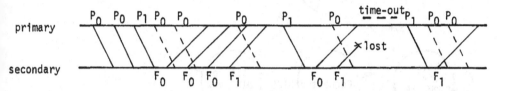

FIGURE 7.16: Example of exchanged HDLC frames in FDX normal response mode

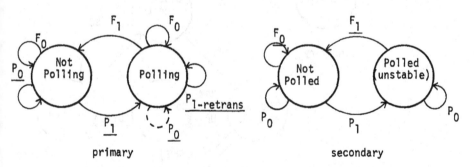

FIGURE 7.17: HDLC asynchronous response mode

168

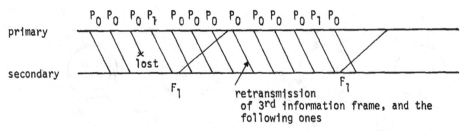

FIGURE 7.18: Example of exchanged HDLC frames in asynchronous response mode

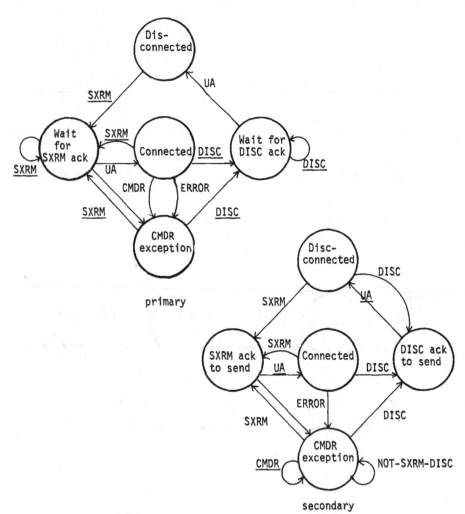

FIGURE 7.19: Unbalanced link set-up procedure (HDLC)

response of the secondary to a particular, previously sent, command frame. The mechanism is specified by the transition diagrams of figure 7.17, which require that the secondary, in response to the reception of a command with the P-bit equal to *one*, immediately sends a frame with the F-bit equal to *one*. This mechanism may be used to determine whether, and from which sequence number, retransmission is required, as shown in the example of figure 7.18.

Balanced class

Two stations communicating according to the balanced class of procedures have equal responsability for the link. They use the asynchronous response mode, described above, and each contains some primary and some secondary functions. The primary function of one station is responsible for the data transfer to the opposite station, and for this purpose, communicates with the secondary function on the other side. To provide the checkpointing function independently in both directions, it is necessary to distinguish between commands (sent by a primary) and responses (sent by a secondary). This is accomplished by using two different station address values (see figure 7.14).

Procedures for link (re-)initialization and disconnection

So far we have considered the data transfer phase. It must be preceded by the so-called "link set-up" phase, which initializes the data transfer protocol. The same initialization procedure may be executed after a procedure error or major transmission failure, in which case it is called a "link reset". To return to the "disconnected" link state, a disconnection procedure may be executed.

In the case of the unbalanced classes, these procedures are initiated by the primary station (for details see figure 7.19), whereas in the balanced case, both stations may initiate them. The initiating station may choose the class of procedure to be used over the link, provided that the chosen class is implemented in both stations involved.

Additional facilities

Without pretending to give a complete description of the
HDLC procedures, we mention below some of the additional functions
foreseen :

(a) Error reporting : An exceptional situation that cannot be
    handled by a station may be reported to the station respon-
    sible by a *command* or *frame reject* frame (CMDR or FRMR).

(b) Selective retransmission is foreseen as an optional facility.

(c) A secondary station may deny the link set-up by responding
    with a DM (*disconnected mode*) frame.

(d) Unnumbered information (UI) frames may be exchanged as an
    optional facility.

7.4.4. *Multiplexing*

In the context of retransmission protocols, multiplexing
means that several logical links, each executing an independent
protocol, share the same underlying transmission service. Each frame
transmitted belongs to one of these links, which is usually identified by an address field. In the case of HDLC, the first octet of
each frame is reserved for the address.

The sharing of the transmission service is managed by
multiplexing and demultiplexing units, as indicated in figure 7.20.
The multiplexing unit selects the logical link which obtains the
right to transmit the next frame to the other side and transmits
the frame after adding the correct address. It may take into account
the states of the different links and distinguish different priorities for deciding the order of transmission. The demultiplexing unit
simply reads the address field, and forwards the frame to the corres
ponding protocol handler.

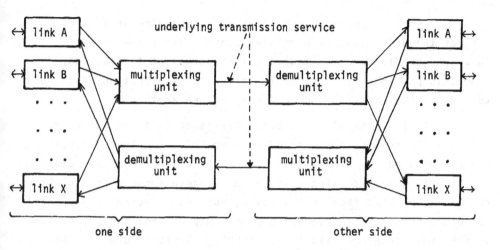

FIGURE 7.20: Multiplexing of several logical links over one transmission service

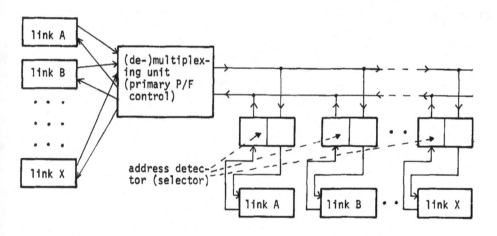

FIGURE 7.21: Multi-point configuration

So far we have assumed that a multiplexing unit on each
side of the underlying transmission service determines the order
in which the different logical links may transmit frames. Apart
from this possible restriction in the speed of execution, the protocols involved operate independently of one another.

In the case of multi-point configurations, as shown in
figure 7.21, this assumption is not true. Usually, there is one
central station to which all logical links connect. At this station
is not only a multiplexing unit which determines the order in which
frames may be sent from that station, but this station also centrally determines the order in which frames may be sent to that station
by the other connected stations. In HDLC, for this purpose, the
normal response mode is used over all links involved such that the
central station contains the primaries. Then the transmission of
frames to the central station is coordinated by polling the other
stations in an appropriate order. To avoid collision conflicts,
only one secondary station of a single link may be polled at any
given time.

FOOTNOTES

1. In a local context, small data blocks (for instance octets
    or memory words) are often presented in parallel, and sepa-
    rate leads are used for signalling flow control or clock
    pulses. Standard interfaces of this kind are described in
    [Knob 75] and [Viss 77].

2. The following description is based on the X.20 interface
    standard for leased circuits.

3. The following is a description of the X.21 standard inter-
    face circuits.

4. For more information about different transmission media and
    communication techniques see for example [Mart 69].

5. The principal techniques use an analogue carrier with phase-
    shift, frequency or amplitude modulation. More about modula-
    tion techniques for data transmission over analogue channels
    may be found in [Mart 69] or [Mart 72].

6. The technology of digital channels is relatively young,
    compared to analogue communication technology. At present,
    digital channels have many advantages over analogue ones,
    especially in relation to data communications and switching
    (electro-mecanical switching centers in telephone networks
    are being replaced by electronic ones).

7. See [HDLC a].

8. The version used in IBM's BSC protocol has become a kind of
    de-facto standard. The following description is based on the
    character-oriented frame format used in [DATAPAC].

9. For a comparison of error correcting codes and error correc-
    tion by retransmission, see for example [Burt 72] .

10. In the case of end-to-end recovery the delay for obtaining acknowledgements or retransmission requests are higher. The effect on the average transmission delay for frames is negligeable if retransmissions are rare. However, there is also an effect on the buffer space required (see footnote 16)

11. For more details, see for example [Mart 70].

12. A similar code is used in certain LSI memories to correct more frequent storage errors.

13. For more details see for example [Gall 68]

14. See for example [Mart 72].

15. Most analysis of protocol efficiency involve simulation studies. See for example [Dant 75] and [Lela 78].

16. The average number of outstanding frames is equal to 2 x D x N, where D is the average transmission delay for packets between the two subsystems, and N is the average number of packets sent per unit time, if we assume that the acknowledgements are returned in packets which are sent immediately.

17. We note that the credit scheme has another advantage over the stop-and-go scheme, namely that it operates over a transmission service which does not guarantee frame sequencing. This is important for end-to-end protocols using a datagram transmission service (see section 6), and for multi-circuit link protocols which use several alternative circuits as transmission service in order to increase the reliability and availability of the logical link [Chun 79], [Jame 78].

18. See for example [Cerf 74].

19. See [Bart 69].

20. The best known example is IBM's BSC protocol used for remote job entry.

21. For more details see [Boch 77] or [Boch 78].

22. See [HDLC b] and [HDLC c]. A more algorithmic, formalized specification is given in [Boch 77 b] (see Annex).

23. Over transmission services with especially long delays, an extended numbering cycle (modulo 128) may be used.

CHAPTER VIII

TECHNOLOGICAL DEVELOPMENTS AND STANDARDS

Due to the advances in the micro-electronic technology, the cost of hardware is drastically decreasing for data processing and communication devices. It is interesting to note that the hardware cost goes down appreciably faster for data processing components, such as memories and processors, than for data communications equipment. This development, therefore, favors future systems which perform data processing at the locations where the data is collected, stored or needed, thus reducing the amount of data transmitted. In most cases these systems will be distributed.

As the hardware costs decrease, more and more system functions will be "realized in hardware" instead of being "programmed in software". The development of specialized hardware may become a discipline similar to the development of system software. The distinction between hardware and software will be become of less importance.

It is important to note that the overall cost of data processing systems will be determined mainly by the cost for designing the hardware and software, which remains essentially constant in time, while the cost for hardware will become relatively small. Therefore it will be very important, and it is already so now, to reduce the amount of design work to be done for any new data processing system.

Modular design, advocated by software engineering approaches such as structured programming, top-down design etc., seems to be necessary for building larger systems in order to avoid a kind of exponential increase of the required design effort. However, it does not reduce the effort needed for designing a given simple module. The only way to reduce this effort seems to be the use of a module which is already built and satisfies the design requirements.

In order to avoid "inventing the wheel" again and again, it is necessary to build software libraries which contain programs of modules which provide frequently-needed functions. To make these modules usable the service provided by each module must be precisely defined, as well as their interface with other modules. It would be useful to develop standards for the most widely used service modules.

The possible reduction of the design effort for new systems is not the only reason for developing standards. The need for interworking between different systems is another important reason. The development of standards for data communication has the main objective of providing a meaningful exchange of data between different systems without requiring ad hoc adaptations between each pair of systems.

The present situation of communication standards is such that reasonable international standards exist for physical interfaces, line protocols and certain network access protocols[1], but for the higher level protocols, including the transport layer, the international discussions are only beginning with the establishment of a layered "Reference Model"[2] which should provide the framework in which higher level function-oriented protocols may be defined. We believe firmly that the adoption of reasonable standards for all functions commonly found in distributed computer system is very important for the present and the future applications of these systems[3].

FOOTNOTES

1. A progress report on data communication standard developments may be found in [Coot 77] .

2. See section 5.2.4.

3. Arguments may be found in [Sand 76] and [Boch 77 c] .

R E F E R E N C E S

[Akko 74]   E.A. Akkoynlu, A.J. Bernstein and R.E. Schwarz,
            "Interprocess communication facilities for network
            operating systems", Computer (IEEE) 7,6 (June 1974),
            pp. 46-55.

[Alsb 77]   P.A. Alsberg and J.D. Day, "A principle for resilient
            sharing of distributed resources", IFIP WG 6.1,
            INWG General Note 127, 1977.

[Ande 75]   G.A. Anderson and E.D. Jensen, "Computer interconnec-
            tion structures : taxonomy, characteristics and exam-
            ples", ACM Computing Surveys 7,4 (Dec. 1975),
            pp. 197-213.

[Ashc 75]   E.A. Ashcroft, "Proving assertions about parallel
            programs", J. Comp. Sys. Sci. 10,1 (Jan. 1975),
            pp. 110-135.

[Aviz 77]   A. Avizienis, "Fault-tolerant computing-progress,
            problems and prospects", Proc. IFIP Congress 1977,
            pp. 405-420.

[Bane 78]   J. Banerjee, D.K. Hsiao and F.K. Ng, "Data network -
            a computer network of general purpose front-end com-
            puters and special-purpose back-end database machines",
            Proc. Computer Network Protocols Symposium, Université
            de Liège, 1978, pp. D6-1 to D6-12.

[Barb 77]   D.L.A. Barber, "The role and nature of a virtual termi-
            nal", ACM Computer Comm. Review 7, 3 (July 1977),
            pp. 5-22.

[Barb 78]   D.L.A. Barber, T. Kalin and C. Solomonides, "An imple-
            mentation of the X.25 interface in a datagram network",
            Proc. Computer Network Protocols Symposium, Université
            de Liège, 1978, pp. E6-1 to E6-5.

[Bart 69]   K.A. Bartlett et al., "A note on reliable full-duplex
            transmission over half-duplex links", Comm. ACM 12, 5
            (May 1969), pp. 260-261

[Bart 77] W. Bartussek and D.L. Parnas, "Using traces to write
abstract specifications for software modules", UNC
Report TR 77-012, University of North Carolina,
Dec. 1977.

[Bekk 77] Y. Bekkers, J. Briat and J.P. Verjus, "Construction
of a synchronization scheme by independent definition
of parallelism", Proc. IFIP Working Conference on
Constructing Quality Software, North-Holland Publ.,
1978, pp. 193-205.

[Belp 75] G. Belpaire, "On programming dependencies between
parallel processes", Techn. Report 244, Comp. Sc. Dept.,
University of Wisconsin, March 1975.

[Bels 78] D. Belsnes, "X.25 DTE implement in Simula", Proc.
Eurocomp 78, 1978, Online, England.

[Bern 77] P.A. Bernstein et al., "The concurrency control mecanism
of SDD-1 : A system for distributed databases", Technical
report, Computer Corp. of America, Cambridge, Mass.,
Dec. 1977.

[Boch 75] G.V. Bochmann, "Logical verification and implementation
of protocols", Proc. Fourth Data Communications Symposium,
ACM/IEEE, 1975, pp. 8-15 to 8-20.

[Boch 76] G.V. Bochmann, "Comments on monitor definition and implementation", Inform. Processing Letters 5,4 (Oct. 1976),
pp. 116-117.

[Boch 77] G.V. Bochmann and J. Gecsei, "A unified model for the
specification and verification of protocols", Proc. IFIP
Congress 1977, North Holland, Amsterdam, 1977,
pp. 229-234.

[Boch 77b] G.V. Bochmann and R.J. Chung, "A formalized description
of HDLC classes of procedures", Proc. National Telecommunications Conference, IEEE, 1977, pp. 03A..2-1 to 2-11.

[Boch 77c] G.V. Bochmann, "Standards issues in data communications",
Telecommunications Policy 1,5 (Dec. 1977), pp. 381-388.

[Boch 77d] G.V. Bochmann, "Synchronization in distributed systems",
Publication 259, Département d'informatique, Université
de Montréal, 1977.

[Boch 77e] G.V. Bochmann, "Combining assertions and states for the
validation of process communication", Proc. IFIP
Working Conference on Constructing Quality Software,
North Holland, 1978, pp. 229-232.

[Boch 78] G.V. Bochmann, "Finite state description of communication
protocols", Computer Networks 2 (Oct. 1978), pp. 361-372.

[Boch 78b] G.V. Bochmann, "Specification and verification of computer communication protocols", submitted to Computer
Networks.

[Boch 78c] G.V. Bochmann and J. Tankoano, "Development and structure of an X.25 implementation", to be published in
IEEE Transactions on SE.

[Boch 79] G.V. Bochmann, "Distributed synchronization and
regularity", Computer Networks 3 (1979), pp. 36-43.

[Boch 80] G.V. Bochmann, "A general transition model for protocols
and communication services", to be published in IEEE
Trans. on Comm.

[Brin 70] P. Brinch-Hansen, "The nucleus of a multiprogramming
system", Comm. ACM 13,4 (April 1970), pp. 238-241, 250.

[Brin 73] P. Brinch-Hansen, "Operating systems principles",
Prentice-Hall, Englewood Cliffs, 1973.

[Brin 75] P. Brinch-Hansen, "The programming language Concurrent
Pascal", IEEE Transactions on Software Eng., SE-1 (1975),
pp. 199-207.

[Burt 72] H.O. Burton and D.D. Sullivan, "Errors and error control",
Proc. of the IEEE, Nov. 1972, pp. 1293-1301.

[Camp 74]   R.H. Campbell and A.N. Habermann, "The specification
            of process synchronization by path expressions", in
            Lecture Notes in Comp. Sc., Vol. 16, Springer, Berlin,
            1974.

[Cave 78]   J.K. Cavers, "Implementation of X.25 on a multiple
            microprocessor system", Proc. Intern. Comm. Conf.,
            1978.

[Cerf 74]   V.G. Cerf and R.E. Kahn, "A protocol for packet network
            intercommunication", IEEE Transactions on Comm., Vol.
            COM-22, 1974, pp. 637-648.

[Chun 79]   R.J. Chung, and A.M. Rybczynski, "Alternatives for
            providing highly reliable access to X.25 networks",
            Proc. NCC79, pp.

[Clip 76]   W.W. Clipsham, "Security in public packet-switching
            networks", Proc. IRIA Workshop on protection and secu-
            rity in data networks, June 1976, Cyclades Report SEC
            021.

[Coff 73]   E.G. Coffmann and P.J. Denning, "Operating systems
            theory", Prentice-Hall, 1973.

[Cott 77]   I.W. Cotton and H.C. Folts, "International standards
            for data communications: a status report", Proc. Fifth
            Data Communications Symposium, ACM/IEEE, 1977, pp. 4-26
            to 4-36.

[Cour 71]   P.J. Courtois et al., "Concurrent control with readers
            and writers", Comm. ACM 14, 10 (Oct. 1971), pp. 667-668.

[Cour 77]   P.J. Courtois, "Decomposability : queuing and computer
            system applications", Academic Press, 1977.

[Cunn 77]   I.M. Cunningham, W.J. Older and A.K. Trividi, "DATAPAC
            software architecture", Bell-Northern Research,
            Febr. 1977.

[Dahl 72]   O.J. Dahl and C.A.R. Hoare, "Hierarchical program
            structures", in Structured Programming, Academic Press,
            1972.

[Dant 76]   A.S. Danthine and J. Bremer, "An axiomatic description
             of the transport protocol of Cyclades", Professional
             Conference on Computer Networks and Teleprocessing,
             TH Aachen, 1976.

[DATAPAC]   The following articles in Proc. International Conference
             on Computer Communications (ICCC), 1976, pp. 129-156
             (a) W.W. Clipsham et al., "Datapac network overview",
                 pp. 131-136.
             (b) S.C.K. Young and C.I. McGibbon, "The control system
                 of the Datapac network", pp. 137-142.
             (c) D.A. Twyver and A.M. Rybczynski, "Datapac subscriber
                 interfaces", pp. 143-149.
             (d) P.M. Cashin, "Datapac network protocols", pp. 150-156.

[Davi 73]   D.W. Davies and D.L.A. Barber, "Communication networks
             for computers", John Wiley & Sons, London, 1973.

[Davi 77]   J. Davidson et al., "The Arpanet Telnet protocol : Its
             purpose, principles, implementation and impact on host
             operating system design", Proc. Fifth Data Communications
             Symposium, ACM/IEEE, 1977, pp. 4-10 to 4-18.

[Depa 76]   M. Deparis et al., "The implementation of an end-to-end
             protocol by EIN centres : a survey and comparison",
             Proc. ICCC, 1976, pp. 351-360.

[Dijk 68]   E.W. Dijkstra, "Cooperating sequential processes", in
             Programming Languages (F. Genuys, ed.), Academic Press,
             1968.

[Dijk 68b]   E.W.D. Dijkstra, "The structure of the THE multiprogram-
             ming system", Comm. ACM 11,5 (May 1968), pp. 341-346.

[Dijk 74]   E.W. Dijkstra, "Self stabilizing systems in spite of
             distributed control", Comm. ACM 17,11 (Nov. 1974),
             pp. 643-644.

[Dijk 75]   E.W. Dijkstra, "Guarded commands, nondeterminacy, and
             formal derivation of programs", Comm. ACM 18,8 (Aug. 1975),
             453-457.

[Doll 72]   D.R. Doll, "Multiplexing and concentration", Proc. IEEE 60,11 (Nov. 1972), pp. 1313-1321.

[Ensl 77]   P.H. Enslow, "Multiprocessor organization - a survey", ACM Computing Surveys 9,1 (March 1977), pp. 103-129.

[Esch 78]   E. Eschenauer and V. Obozinski, "The network communication manager : a transport station for the SGB Network", Computer Networks 2 (1978), pp. 236-249.

[Farb 75]   D.J. Farber and K.C. Larson, "Network security via dynamic process renaming", Proc. Fourth Data Communications Symposium, ACM/IEEE, 1975, pp. 8-13 to 8-18.

[Floy 67]   R.W. Floyd, "Assigning meaning to programs", Proc. Symp. in Applied Mathematics, Vol. 19 (1967), American Math. Soc., pp. 19-32.

[Gall 68]   R.G. Gallanger, "Information theory and reliable communication" (chapt. 6.8), Wiley, 1968.

[Gien 78]   M. Gien, "A file transfer protocol", Proc. Computer Network Protocol Symposium, Université de Liège, 1978, pp. D5-1 to D5-7.

[Goos 72]   G. Goos, J. Jürgens and K. Lagally, "The operating system BSM viewed as a community of parallel processes", Abteilung Mathematik der TU München, Bericht Nr. 7208, 1972.

[Goud 76]   M.G. Gouda and E.G. Manning, "Protocol machines : a concise formal model and its automatic implementation", Proc. ICCC, 1976, pp. 346-350.

[HDLC a]   ISO, IS 3309, "Data communication - HDLC - frame structure".

[HDLC b]   ISO, DIS 4335 and 1445, "Data communication - HDLC - elements of procedure".

[HDLC c]   ISO, DIS 6159 and 6256, HDLC unbalanced and balanced classes of procedures.

[Hech 76]   H. Hecht, "Fault-tolerant software for real-time applications", ACM Computing Surveys 8,4 (Dec. 1976), pp. 391-408.

[Hert 78] F. Hertweck et al., "X.25 based process-process communication", Computer Networks 2 (1978), pp. 250-270.

[Hoar 69] C.A.R. Hoare, "An axiomatic basis for computer programming", Comm. ACM 12,10 (Oct. 1969), pp. 576-580.

[Hoar 74] C.A.R. Hoare, "Monitors : an operating systems structuring concept", Comm. ACM 17,10 (Oct. 1974), pp. 549-557.

[Hoar 78] C.A.R. Hoare, "Communicating sequential processes", Comm. ACM 21,8 (Aug. 1978), pp. 666-677.

[Hobb 72] L.C. Hobbs, "Terminals", Proc. IEEE 60,11 (Nov. 1972), pp. 1273-1284.

[Holt 70] A.W. Holt and F. Commoner, "Events and conditions", in Project MAC Conference on Concurrent Systems and Parallel Computation, June 1970.

[Horn 73] J.J. Horning and B. Randell, "Process structuring", ACM Computing Surveys 5,1 (March 1973), pp. 5-30.

[INWG 78] IFIP WG6.1, "Proposal for an internetwork end-to-end transport protocol", INWG General Note ≠ 96.1, Febr. 1978.

[Jame 78] B. Jamet and G. Mainguenaud, "A multi-line data link control procedure", Proc. ICCC-78 (1978), pp.289-294.

[Jamm 77] A.J. Jammel and H.G. Stiegler, "Managers versus monitors", Proc. IFIP Congress 1977, pp. 827-830.

[Jenn 77] C.J. Jenny, "Process partitioning in distributed systems", Proc. Nat. Telecomm. Conf., Los Angeles, 1977.

[Kahn 72] R.E. Kahn, "Resource-sharing computer communications networks", Proc. IEEE 60,11 (Nov. 1972), pp. 1397-1407.

[Kahn 74] G. Kahn, "The semantics of a simple language for parallel programming", Proc. IFIP Congress 1974, pp. 471-475.

[Karp 69] R. Karp and R.E. Miller, "Parallel program schemata", Journal of Comp. and Systems Sci. 3, pp. 147-195 (1969).

[Kell 76] R.M. Keller, "Formal verification of parallel programs",
           Comm. ACM 19,7 (July 1976), pp. 371-384.

[Kess 77] J.L.W. Kessels, "An alternative to event queues for
           synchronization in monitors", Comm. ACM 20,7 (July 1977),
           pp. 500-503.

[Kirs 76] P.J. Kirstein, "Planned new public data networks", Compu-
           ter Networks 1,2 (Sept. 1976).

[Klei 75] L. Kleinrock, "Queuing systems", Vol. I : Theory,
           Vol. II : Computer applications, Wiley, 1975-76.

[Knob 75] D.E. Knoblock et al., "Insight into interfacing", IEEE
           Spectrum, May 1975.

[Lamp 73] B. Lampson, "A note of the confinement problem", Comm.
           ACM 16,10 (Oct. 1973), pp. 613-615.

[Lamp 74] L. Lamport, "A new solution of Dijkstra's concurrent
           programming problem", Comm. ACM 17,8 (August 1974),
           pp. 453-455.

[Lamb 78] L. Lamport, "Time, clocks and the ordering of events
           in a distributed system", Comm. ACM 21,7 (July 1978),
           pp. 558-565.

[Laue 75] P.E. Lauer and R.H. Campbell, "Formal semantics of a
           class of high-level primitives for coordinating
           concurrent processes", Acta Informatica 5 (1975)
           pp. 297-332.

[Lela 77] G. LeLann, "Distributed systems - towards a formal
           approach", Proc. IFIP Congress 1977, pp. 155-160.

[Lela 78] G. LeLann and H. LeGoff, "Verification and evaluation
           of communication protocols", Computer Networks 2,1
           (Febr. 1978), pp. 50-69.

[Lind 76] T.A. Linden, "Operating system structures to support
           security and reliable software", ACM Computing surveys
           8,4 (Dec. 1976), pp. 409-445.

[Lipt 74]   R.J. Lipton, L. Snyder and Y. Zalcstein, "A comparative
            study of models of parallel computation, "Proc. 15th
            Annual Symp. Switching and Automata, IEEE, NY, 1974,
            pp. 145-155.

[Lisk 75]   B. Liskov and S. Zilles, "Specification techniques for
            data abstractions", IEEE Trans. on Software Engineering
            1,1 (March 1975), pp. 7-18.

[Mart 69]   J. Martin, "Telecommunications and the computer",
            Prentice-Hall, 1969.

[Mart 70]   J. Martin, "Teleprocessing network organization",
            Prentice-Hall, 1970.

[Mart 72]   J. Martin, "Systems analysis for data transmission",
            Prentice-Hall, 1972.

[Mart 77]   J.G. Martins, "Communication implicite entre des pro-
            cessus répartis sur un réseau hétérogène", Thèse DEA,
            INPG, Grenoble, Sept. 1977.

[Masu 78]   Y. Masunaga, "A probabilistic automaton model of the
            NRM, HDX HDLC procedure", Computer Networks 2,6
            (Dec. 1978), pp. 442-453.

[Mell 77]   F. Mellor, W.J. Olden and C.J. Bedard, "A message-
            switched operating system for a multiprocessor",
            Proc. COMPSAC 77 (IEEE Chicago, 1977), pp. 772-777.

[Mena 79]   D.A. Menasce and R.R. Muntz, "Locking and deadlock
            detection in distributed databases", IEEE Trans.
            SE, to appear.

[Merl 76]   P.M. Merlin, "A methodology for the design and imple-
            mentation of communication protocols", IEEE Transactions
            on Comm., Vol. COM-24, 1976, pp. 614-621.

[Merl 76b] P.M. Merlin and D.J. Farber, "Recoverability of commu-
            nication protocols-implications of a theoretical study",
            IEEE Transact. on Comm., Sept. 1976, pp. 1036-1043.

[Merl 77]   P.M. Merlin and A. Segall, "A failsafe algorithm for
            loop-free distributed routing in data-communication
            networks", to be published in IEEE Transactions on
            Comm.

[Merl 77b] P.M. Merlin and B. Randell, "Consistant state restoration in distributed systems", to be published in Comm. ACM.

[Metc 76] R.M. Metcalfe and D.R. Boggs, "Ethernet : distributed packet switching for local computer networks", Comm. ACM 16,7 (July 1976), pp. 395-404.

[Moss 77] J. Mossière et al., "Sur l'exclusion mutuelle dans les réseaux informatiques", Publication interne No 75, IRISA, Rennes.

[Nayl 75] W.E. Naylor, "A loop-free adaptive routing algorithm for packet switched networks", Proc. Fourth Data Communications Symposium, ACM/IEEE, 1975, pp. 7-9 to 7-14.

[Need 78] R.M. Needham and M.D. Schroeder, "Using encryption for authentication in large networks of computers", Comm. ACM 21,12 (Dec. 1978), pp. 993-999.

[Noe 73] J.D. Noe and G.J. Nutt, "Macro E-Nets for representation of parallel systems", IEEE Trans. Comp. C-22,8 (Aug. 1973), 718-727.

[Parn 74] D.L. Parnas, "On a "buzzword" : hierarchical structure", Proc. IFIP Congress 1974, pp. 336-339.

[Parn 77] D.L. Parnas, "The use of precise specifications in the development of software", Proc. IFIP Congress 1977, pp. 861-867.

[Pete 74] J.L. Peterson and T.H. Bredt, "A comparison of models of parallel computation", Proc. IFIP Congress 1974, North-Holland, Amsterdam, 1974, pp. 466-470.

[Pete 77] J.L. Peterson, "Petri nets", ACM Computing survey 9,3 (Sept. 1977), pp. 223-252.

[Pouz 73] L. Pouzin, "Presentation and major design aspects of the Cyclades computer network", Proc. Third Data Communications Symposium, ACM/IEEE, 1973, pp. 80-87.

[Prob 77]   W.G. Probst and G.V. Bochmann, "Operating systems design
            with computer network communication protocols",
            Proc. Fifth Data Communications Symposium, ACM/IEEE,
            1977, pp. 4-19 to 4-25.

[Rand 75]   B. Randell, "System structure for software fault-
            tolerance", Proc. International Conf. on Reliable Soft-
            ware, IEEE/ACM, 1975, pp. 437-449.

[Redz 77]   R.R. Redziejowski, "Parallel processes and languages
            with infinite words", submitted to J. ACM, March 1977.

[Ridd 72]   W.E. Riddle, "The modeling and analysis of supervisory
            systems", PhD thesis, Computer Sc. Dept., Stanford
            University, March 1972.

[Robe 70]   L.G. Roberts and B.D. Wessler, "Computer network
            development to achieve resource sharing", Proc. SJCC,
            AFIPS, 1970, pp. 543-549.

[Robe 77]   P. Robert and J.P. Verjus, "Toward autonomous descrip-
            tions of synchronization modules", Proc. IFIP Congress
            1977, pp. 981-986.

[Rybc 77]   A.M. Rybczynski and D.F. Weir, "Datapac X.25 service
            characteristics", Proc. Fifth Data Communications
            Symposium, ACM/IEEE, 1977, pp. 4-50 to 4-57.

[Sand 76]   R.W. Sanders and V. Cerf, "Compatibility or chaos in
            communications", Datamation, March 1976.

[Sevc 72]   K.C. Sevcick et al., "Project SUE as a learning expe-
            rience", Proc. FJCC 1972, AFIPS 41, p. 331.

[Shoc 78]   J.F. Shoch, "Inter-network naming, addressing and
            routing", Proc. IEEE Compcon 78, Sept. 1978, pp. 72-79.

[Simo 62]   H.A. Simon, "The architecture of complexity", Proc.
            American Philosophical Society 106 (1962), pp. 468-482.

[Somm 76]   R. Sommer, "COBUS, a firmware controlled data trans-
            mission system", Proc. 2nd Symposium on Micro Architec-
            ture, 1976, North Holland Publ. Comp., pp. 299-304.

[Sten 76] N.V. Stenning, "A data transfer protocol", Computer
           Networks 1, 1976, pp. 99-110

[Thom 76] R.H. Thomas, "A solution to the update problem for
           multiple copy data bases which uses distributed control",
           Bolt Beranek and Newman Inc., Report No 3340, July 1976.

[Viss 77] C.A. Vissers, "Interface : Definition, design and des-
           cription of the relation of digital system parts",
           Technische Hogeschool Twente, The Netherlands, 1977.

[Whit 78] C. Whitby-Strevens, "Towards the performance evaluation
           of distributed computing systems", to be presented at
           IEEE COMPSAC, Chicago, Nov. 1978.

[Wirt 77] N. Wirth, "Toward a discipline of real-time programming",
           Comm. ACM 20,8 (Aug. 1977), pp. 577-583.

[Wirt 77b] N. Wirth, "Modula : a language for modular multiprogram-
           ming", Softw. Pract. Experience 7,1 (Jan-Feb. 1977),
           pp. 3-35.

[Wulf 74] W.A. Wulf et al., "HYDRA : the kernel of a multi-
           processor operating system", Comm. ACM 17,6 (June 1974),
           pp. 337-345.

[Zimm 75] H. Zimmermann, "The Cyclades end-to-end protocol", Proc.
           Fourth Data Communications Symposium, ACM/IEEE, 1975,
           pp. 7-21 to 7-26.

ANNEX 1

A N N E X

AN EXAMPLE OF A PROTOCOL IMPLEMENTATION

BASED ON A FORMALIZED SPECIFICATION.

In order to give a realistic example for the use of formal specification methods during the design and implementation of communication protocols, we include in this annex some papers which relate to the formalized specification of the HDLC classes of procedures (see section 7.4.3) and their implementation in a high-level programming language.

The first two papers describe the specification formalism which uses state transition diagrams and programming language elements, as explained in section 4.7. They also use the induction principle (see section 4.6) for verifying protocols (see also section 5.4), and take the simple "alternating bit" protocol (see section 7.4.2) as an example. The third paper shows (in its Appendix) how certain aspects of the service provided by a link layer protocol (see section 5.2.1), and in particular HDLC, may be formally specified. The following paper gives a formalized specification of the HDLC classes of procedures. This specification was taken as the basis for the implementation of the X.25 link layer in Concurrent Pascal, which is described in the last paper.

A1. "A unified model for the specification and verification of protocols" (by G.V. Bochmann and J. Gecsei [Boch 77]), which appeared in Information Processing 77, North-Holland Publ. Company.

A2. "Combining assertions and states for the validation of process communication" [Boch 77 e], which appeared in Constructing Quality Software, North-Holland Publ. Company.

A3. "Defining a layer service", extract from a Canadian contribution to ISO TC97/SC 16 (1979).

193

A4. "A formalized description of HDLC classes of procedures"
(by G.V. Bochmann and R.J. Chung [Boch 77 b]), which was
presented at the IEEE National Telecommunications Conference,
1977.

A5. "Development and structure of an X.25 implementation"
(by G.V. Bochmann and T. Joachim [Boch 78 c]), to be
published in IEEE Transactions on Software Engineering.

   We thank the respective publishers for the kind permission
to include these papes.

A UNIFIED METHOD FOR THE SPECIFICATION AND VERIFICATION OF PROTOCOLS*

GREGOR V. BOCHMANN and JAN GECSEI
Département d'informatique, Université de Montréal
Montréal, Canada

Verification of communication protocols usually involves two parts: a state-machine analysis of the control structure and proving some assertions about the semantic content of the protocol's actions. The two parts are traditionally treated separately. This paper suggests that the two approaches are not independent but rather complementary. It introduces a unified model for protocols (and generally cooperating distant subsystems) encompassing both aspects. The method is demonstrated on three different descriptions of the same protocol, each with a different tradeoff between state machine and programming aspects. Verification of partial and full correctness is carried out in terms of the three descriptions.

1. INTRODUCTION

Experience with design and logical verification of communication protocols indicates that various techniques are suitable for the verification of different properties of the same protocol. All known verification techniques derive in some way from two fundamental approaches: the state machine approach [1,2] and the programming language approach. [3,4] The first of these has been used when the properties of the protocol to be verified are such as the absence of deadlocks or undesired loops or proper sequencing of operations. The programming language approach is used with properties involving counting and, in general, in cases when the state machine representations would become too complex (involve too many states).

The state-machine techniques use always some form of reachability analysis, whereas the programming language method relies on proving assertions and invariants [5] and normally does not address the question of reachability or termination.

It would seem, at first, that there is little connection between the state-machine and programming language approaches to verification. This is partly because both methodologies have their own established formalism, quite different one from another. Thus, attempts to establish a bridge between the methodologies may be frustrated by the necessity to pass from one formalism to the other, which is not always trivial.

It is our belief that the two approaches to verification are not independent, but rather complementary techniques. In order to benefit maximally from both methods, they should be used together; but it is first necessary to create a model that incorporates both the state machine and programming language formalisms. Such a model is described in sections 2 and 3. We believe that this model is widely applicable to the specification and verification of systems of communicating processes. In order to show its usefulness, we have chosen a particular system, a simple data communication protocol working over an unreliable transmission medium, for which we present three different specifications in section 4. In section 5 we demonstrate how some correctness proofs can be carried out for the three descriptions.

*This work has been partly supported by the National Research Council of Canada.

2. THE BASIC MODEL

In a recent paper, Keller [6] has proposed a model for the representation of parallel programs. His model is essentially a Petri net [7] composed of a set of places and transitions complemented with a set of variables X. Each transition t in the net has associated with it an enabling predicate P_t, depending on some variables of X, and an action A_t, assigning new values to some variables of X. The state of the modeled system is determined by the number of tokens that reside in different places and the values of the variables. A certain transition t of the system is enabled when all its input places have at least one token (standard rule for Petri nets) and its enabling predicate P_t is true. When a transition is enabled, it may fire, i.e. the corresponding action A_t is executed, and the tokens are redistributed according to the rules of Petri nets.

In the original model all transitions and actions are assumed to be instantaneous, which implies their mutual exclusion.

Keller's model is intuitively appealing since it is capable of naturally representing some important aspects of the systems being modeled:

- control structure is represented by the interconnection of places, transitions and some variables of the set X

- semantic structure is represented by the variables, predicates and actions associated with transitions

- parallelism and coordination can be modeled by having several transitions enabled at the same time. The number of tokens in the model is generally not limited.

3. THE EXTENDED MODEL

In Keller's model each variable can, in principle, be affected by all transitions in the system. For the description of distributed systems which consist of several communicating subsystems located at different points in space, it seems to be natural that local variables of a given subsystem can only be affected by the transitions of that subsystem. We therefore extend Keller's model to include the possibility of having several disjoint subsystems and some means of communication between them as follows.

A system S (i.e. parallel program) is composed of a number of subsystems $S_1, S_2, \ldots, S_n$. Each subsystem, separately, is modeled by the formalism of the previous section. If the set of variables of subsystem S_i is called X_i (the <u>local</u> variables of S_i), then the predicates and actions (called <u>local</u> actions) of the subsystem X_i only refer to these local variables.

For the interaction of different subsystems, each subsystem may contain certain <u>distantly initiated actions</u>. Like the local actions, they may assign new values to the local variables; however, they are not associated with a given transition of the subsystem. Distantly initiated actions are <u>executed</u> some finite time after they have been <u>initiated</u> by a distant subsystem; this is done by the execution of an initiating statement in a local action of the distant subsystem. The initiating subsystem may pass value parameters for the execution of the distantly initiated action. All actions in a subsystem are executed in mutual exclusion.

This form of interaction between subsystems seems to capture the essential properties of subsystem communication through the exchange of messages. In fact, the initiation of an action in a distant subsystem corresponds to the sending of a message (the action parameters are the message content), and the execution of the distantly initiated action corresponds to the receiving of the message by the distant subsystem.

We note that the <u>state of the system</u>, at a given instant in time when no action is being executed, is given by the states of all subsystems, i.e. their token distribution and variable values, and the set of distant action initiations which have not yet been executed. The latter set can be understood as the state of the "communication medium", or the messages "in transit".

We also remark that the set of variables X_i together with all actions defined in S_i constitute an abstract data type with mutual exclusion of the actions. [8]

For the specification of the variable declarations, predicates and actions of a subsystem, we use a notation close to the programming language Pascal. [9] Initiation of a distant action can be achieved by the primitive INITIATE $< name, p_1, \ldots, p_k >$ appearing as a statement in a local action, which specifies the name of a unique distantly initiated action and k parameter values. We note that the initiating action does not wait for the completion of the initiated action, and that the order of execution of several distantly initiated actions may be different from the order in which they were initiated.

4. EXAMPLES

In this section we show the flexibility of the extended model by giving three descriptions of the same protocol: the first and second minimizing the number of places and variables respectively, and the third having a certain balance between them.

The protocol we use is essentially the "alternating bit" protocol of Bartlett [10] which can be summarized as follows:

. It is a point-to-point protocol using the communication medium alternatively in both directions.

. In contrast to [10] we suppose data transfer in one direction only, from the SENDER subsystem to the RECEIVER subsystem.

. The SENDER waits for an acknowledge message before the next data message is sent.

. The protocol recovers from transmission errors detected by a redundancy check, and from lost messages through a time-out mechanism in the SENDER. In both cases, retransmission of the data message occurs.

4.1 One-place description

(a) <u>Place diagram</u>   SENDER

Initial state   Send   Clock

— seq=1; ack=1

(b) <u>Variables</u>: Same as three-place description

(c) <u>Actions</u>

Transition	enabling predicate	action
Send	ack≠none ∨ tout=true	if ack=seq then begin new(data); seq:= seq+1(mod2); end; INITIATE (transD,seq,data); ack:=none; time:=t_o; tout:=false;
Clock transA(p:(0,1)) } same as three-place description		

(a) <u>Place diagram</u>   RECEIVER

Initial state   Receive

— exp=1; seqnb=none

(b) <u>Variables</u>: Same as three-place description

(c) <u>Actions</u>

Transition	enabling predicate	action
Receive	seqnb≠none	if seqnb=exp+1(mod2) then begin use(data); exp:=exp+1 (mod2); end; INITIATE (transA, exp); seqnb:=none;
transD(p_1:(0,1),p_2:…)		same as three-place description

4.2 Six-place description

(a) Place diagrams

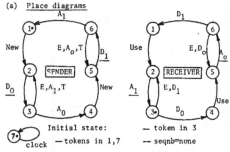

Initial state: — token in 3   —tokens in 1,7   -- seqnb=none

(b) <u>Variables</u>: same as in three-state description except that seq and exp are no longer needed as a consequence of the "unfolded" place diagrams.

(c) <u>Actions</u>: There would be an action (possibly empty) associated with each transition. We do not include a detailed list, since they are analogous to those of the 3-place description.

4.3 Three-place description

(a) Place diagram — SENDER

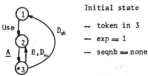

Initial state:
— tokens in 1,4
— seq = 1

New
A
D
E, A≠
T
Clock

(b) Variables

Variables	Meaning
seq: (0,1)	sequence number of message sent in this cycle
ack: (0,1,error,none)	acknowledge from receiver
data: . . .	data to be transmitted
tout: boolean	time-out has occurred
time: integer	timer count

(c) Actions

transition	enabling predicate	action	meaning
New	true	new(data);seq:=seq+1(mod2);	get new data from user
D	true	INITIATE(transD,seq,data); ack:=none;time:=t_0 ; tout:=false;	transmit message (seq,data)
A=	ack=seq	;	reception of expected acknowledge
A≠	ack=seq+1 (mod2)	;	reception of wrong acknowledge
E	ack=error	;	error in received acknowledge
T	tout=true	;	timeout has occurred
Clock	true	time:=time-1;if time=0 then tout:=true ;	timer action
distantly initiated action transA (p:(0,1))			depending on the transmission medium, one of the following will occur:
		case transmission of correct:ack:=p;	acknowledge received
		erroneous:ack:=error;	erroneous reception
		loss :;	message lost

(a) Place diagram — RECEIVER

1
Use
D≠
2
A
E,D=
3

Initial state
— token in 3
— exp = 1
— seqnb = none

(b) Variables

Variables	Meaning
exp: (0,1)	opposite of expected sequence number of message received in this cycle
seqnb: (0,1,error,none)	sequence number of received message
data: . . .	data in received message

(c) Actions

transition	enabling predicate	action	meaning
Use	true	use(data);exp:=exp+1(mod2);	give data to user
A	true	INITIATE (transA, exp); seqnb:=none;	transmit message (exp) (= acknowledge)
D≠	seqnb=exp+1 (mod2)	;	reception of message with expected sequence number
D=	seqnb=exp	;	reception of message with wrong sequence number
E	seqnb=error	;	error in received message
distantly initiated action transD(p_1:(0,1);p_2:...)			depending on the transmission medium, one of the following will occur:
		case transmission of correct:seqnb:=p_1; data:=p_2;	message received
		erroneous: seqnb:= error	erroneous reception
		loss :;	message lost

4.4 Comments

The purpose of the preceding examples is to demonstrate that places and variables are complementary means of representing the state of communicating subsystems. The correctness proofs outlined in the following section are based on both aspects of the formalism we use.

We note, however that in these examples the full power of Petri nets is not used; it is not clear to us at this point whether this power is useful in modeling communication protocols. The idea of using finite state machines and variables for protocol description is not new; [11] however, our approach incorporates also a means for describing communications, which leads to a unified proof methodology.

It should be clear also that the concept of distantly initiated actions can serve equally for modeling of more general communication systems such as the datagram service, or communicating processes in operating systems.

5. VERIFICATION

We demonstrate in this section how the modeling technique described previously can be used for the verification of different properties of a protocol such as absence of deadlocks, liveness, cyclic behavior, partial and full correctness of the global system. Of course these properties are not mutually independent; however, the first four, generally, are necessary conditions for the last one.

Deadlock-freeness, liveness and cyclic behavior are best derived from an analysis of possible transitions of the global system i.e. the reachability analysis. [1,2] This in turn requires taking into account the control structures of each subsystem, certain constraints on the order in which transitions and distantly initiated actions can be executed, and some assertions on program variables.

Verification of partial correctness [5] will correspond in this paper to finding out whether and in which circumstances the sender subsystem (and its user) can "know" that all data obtained from the user have been delivered correctly and in sequence to the user in the receiver subsystem. This knowledge can be expressed by the predicate

P_1 : Producer-sequence = Consumer-sequence.

We say that the sender is in a complete state when this state implies P_1 . Partial correctness of the system means then the existence of a complete sender state, and full correctness means that such a state is always reached after a finite amount of time (liveness of the complete sender state and absence of deadlocks).

We show in section 5.2 that for the three-state description (see section 4.3) of the "alternating bit" protocol the sender state "token in place 1" is complete. Similarly for the one- and six-place descriptions the sender states "$ack = seq$" and "token in place 1 or place 4" respectively, are complete.

5.1 Possible transitions of the global system in the three-place model

Before constructing a transition graph, we have to point out the existence of the following constraint: the predicates and actions of the sender subsystem are defined such that after the execution of transition D (containing $ack:=none$), the transitions $A_=$, $A_{\neq}$ or E can only become enabled after execution of the distantly initiated action $transA$ with correct or erroneous transmission. A similar

constraint holds for the receiver. We also see that the time-out transition can only occur after the timer has been set by transition D and t_o clock transitions have occurred.

We can now determine the possible transitions of the global system as shown in the diagram of fig. 1. Each state $\langle pl_1, pl_2\rangle$ action of the global system is characterized by the active places pl_1 and pl_2 (containing a token) of the sender and receiver subsystem respectively and, possibly, by a distantly initiated action not yet executed. The details of deriving such diagrams have been presented elsewhere. [2] Briefly, it is based on the control structure of the subsystems, on the constraints mentioned above, on the fact that the actions $transA$ and $transD$ are initiated (only) by the A and D transitions of the receiver and sender respectively, and on the initial state of the system.

We have assumed that the time-out delay t_o could be chosen such that the time-out transition ^oT will only occur after a transmission loss has occurred. This clearly depends on the execution speeds and delays of the different transitions and distantly activated actions. We have not included these considerations [1] in our model.

We can conclude from fig. 1 that the constraints mentioned above do not introduce any deadlock (each state has a successor) and that the system shows a cyclic behavior such as expected for a data transmission protocol.

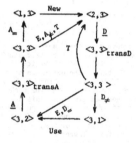

Fig. 1. Possible transitions of the global system (three-place description)

5.2 Verification of partial and full correctness of the three-place description

We can establish the following assertions

AS_1 : sender token in place 3 $\wedge$
    sender.ack=0 or 1

$\Rightarrow$ sender.ack = receiver.exp

AS_2 : receiver token in place 3 $\wedge$
    receiver.seqnb=0 or 1

$\Rightarrow$ receiver.seqnb = sender.seq $\wedge$
    receiver.data = sender.data

which are used below for proving the partial and full correctness. Assertion AS_1 follows from the fact that when ack = 0 or 1 in place 3 then the action $transA$ must have been executed since the sender has entered place 3. However, the receiver uses the value of exp as an effective parameter for initializing the action *transA* and the receiver could not have done any further transition (see fig. 1) thus leaving the variable *exp* unchanged. The assertion AS_2 can be shown similarly.

Now we define the following global predicates:

P_1 : Producer-sequence=Consumer-sequence (as above)

P_2 : Producer-sequence=Consumer-sequence | sender.data (where the " | " means concatenation)

P_3 : sender.seq = receiver.exp

and establish the invariant assertion

I : $(P_1 \wedge P_3) \vee (P_2 \wedge \neg P_3)$, which is proved by induction over the number of transitions executed. Initially $(P_1 \wedge P_3)$ holds, which implies I. Suppose now that I holds in some given state of the system; we have to show that I also holds after one of the subsystems has executed a transition or a distantly activated action. We note that the distantly activated actions do not affect the predicates P_1, P_2 or P_3, neither do the transitions, except the *New* transition of the sender and the *Use* transition of the receiver.

The following arguments show that I is invariant in respect to the execution of the transition *New*; similar arguments apply for the transition *Use*. From AS_1 and the enabling predicate of the transition $A_=$ in the sender follows that P_3 holds when a token is in place 1. Together with I, this implies that P_1 holds in place 1. We now consider the axiomatic definition [5]

$$Q \begin{matrix} \text{Producer-sequence} \\ \text{Producer-sequence} \mid \text{data} \end{matrix} \left\{ \text{new (data)} \right\} Q$$

for the procedure *new*, which means that for proving an assertion Q to hold after the execution of the statement "new (data)", it is sufficient to prove that Q' holds before the execution of the statement, where Q' is obtained from Q by substituting "Producer-sequence | data" for each occurrence of "Producer-sequence" in Q . This definition, together with the form of the action associated with the transition *New* shows that $(P_2 \wedge \neg P_3)$ holds after the execution of *New*, which implies that I holds, too. Therefore I is invariant in respect to the transition *New*.

As mentioned above, the invariant I implies that P_1 holds when the sender is in place 1. Therefore this is a complete state, which implies the partial correctness of the protocol.

Now, in order to demonstrate its full correctness, we have to show that the complete sender state indicated above is live. This can be seen from fig. 2 which shows the diagram of possible transitions of the global system, where, in contrast to fig. 1, we distinguish the states for which P_3 holds (indicated by a " = ") and those for which $\neg P_3$ holds (indicated by a " $\neq$ "). The transition diagram shows that the state < 1,3 > , corresponding to the complete state of the sender, lies on the main loop which is always followed when the transmission medium works correctly. We note that in this case the transitions $A_=$ and $D_{\neq}$ will never be blocked (see AS_1 and AS_2). Therefore the complete sender state is live as long as there is no permanent malfunction of the transmission medium.

5.3 Verification of the one-place protocol description

The verification follows the same lines as for the three-place description. The assertions corresponding to AS_1 and AS_2 are

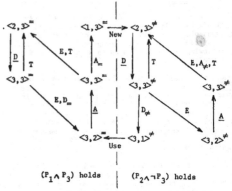

Fig. 2. Possible transitions of the global system (three-place description, distinguishing states with respect to P_3)

AS_1' : sender.ack = 0 or 1

$\Rightarrow$ sender.ack = receiver.exp

AS_2' : receiver.seqnb = 0 or 1

$\Rightarrow$ receiver.seqnb = sender.seq $\wedge$ receiver.data = sender.data

and the invariant I is the same as before.

We note that the diagram of possible transitions for the global system in this case does not contain much information, since each subsystem has essentially only one place. This implies, in particular, that the proof of the liveness of the complete sender state is not as clear as in the case of the three-place description.

5.4 Verification of the six-place protocol description

The verification follows similar lines as for the one- and three-place descriptions. The analysis of possible transitions of the global system yields the diagram of fig. 3. The only assertion used is AS_2: "receiver token in place 1 or 4 $\Rightarrow$ receiver.data = sender.data" and corresponds to assertion AS_2 of the three-place description. There is no invariant, but either P_1 or P_2 hold depending on the places of the sender and receiver tokens (see fig. 3). From this follows that the sender is in a complete state when a token is in place 1 or 4.

We note that the diagram of fig. 3 is equivalent to the one of fig. 2, except that for the six-place description each state in fig. 2 is replicated twice, once for the value of *seq* = 0 and once for *seq* = 1. We see that in this case [12] the reachability analysis that yields fig. 3 provides the proof of the liveness of the complete sender state, as well as the essential part of the "partial correctness" proof.

6. CONCLUSIONS

We have shown that the two complementary approaches of state machine models and the use of variables can be combined into a unified method for the specification and verification of systems of cooperating subsystems. Our unified model includes also the con-

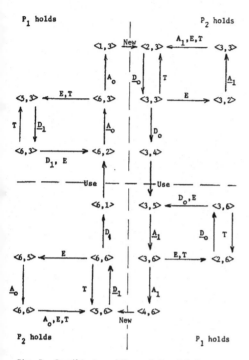

P$_1$ holds   P$_2$ holds

P$_2$ holds   P$_1$ holds

Fig. 3. Possible transitions of the global
system (six-place description)

REFERENCES

[·1] P.M. Merlin, A methodology for the design and
implementation of communication protocols,
IEEE Transactions on Comm., Vol. COM-24,
1976, 614-621.

[2] G.V. Bochmann, Finite state description of
communication protocols, Publication # 236,
Dép. d'Informatique, Univ. de Montréal,
July 1976.

[3] G.V. Bochmann, Logical verification and implementation of protocols, Proc. Fourth Data
Communications Symposium ACM/IEEE, 1975.

[4] N.V. Stenning, A data transfer protocol,
Computer Networks 1 1976, 99-110.

[5] C.A.R. Hoare, An axiomatic basis for computer
programming, CACM, 12, 1969.

[6] R.M. Keller, Formal verification of Parallel
programs, CACM, 7, 1976, 371-384.

[7] A.W. Holt and F. Commoner, Events and conditions, in Project Mac conference on Concurrent
Systems and Parallel Computation, June 1970.

[8] B.H. Liskov and S.N. Zilles, Specification
techniques for data abstractions, IEEE Trans.
on Software Engineering, SE-1, p. 7, 1975.

[9] K. Jensen and N. Wirth, Pascal user manual
and report, Springer Verlag, Berlin, 1974.

[10] K.A. Bartlett, R.A. Scantlebury and P.T. Wilkinson, A note on reliable full-duplex transmission over half-duplex links, CACM 12, 260,
1969.

[11] A.S. Danthine, J. Bremer, An axiomatic des-
cription of the transport protocol of
Cyclades, Professional Conference on Computer
Networks and Teleprocessing, TH Aachen,
March 1976.

[12] G.V. Bochmann, Communication protocols and
error recovery procedures, Proc. ACM Inter-
process Communications Workshop, March 1975.
Op. Syst. Review, Vol. 9, No. 3, 45-50.

cept of distantly initiated actions, which seems to
be useful for modeling the communication of subsystems through the exchange of messages.

We have demonstrated the flexibility of the model by
giving three different specifications for the same
simple protocol. We believe that the model can also
provide a natural description of more complex protocols. For example, the opening and closing of connections are usually described by a state machine
model, whereas the data transfer phase is described
by a program model with variables. [4] With our
model, both aspects could be described in a unique
specification.

For the verification, the two aspects of our model
complement one another. As shown in the example
in the previous sections, the program aspect provides assertions for correctness proofs, whereas the
state machine aspect provides useful information for
the former and facilitates the proof of liveness or
absence of deadlocks.

There is clearly a tradeoff between the complexity
of the state machine and program aspects of the specification, as can be seen, for example, from the
comparison of the one-place and six-place descriptions. Since reachability analysis of state machines seems to be more amenable to algorithmic
methods than verifying (and finding) program assertions, the above tradeoff may have important
implications for future automated methods of protocol verification.

ANNEX   2

Constructing Quality Software, P.G. Hibbard/S.A. Schuman (eds.)
©IFIP, North-Holland Publishing Company, (1978)

COMBINING ASSERTIONS AND STATES FOR THE VALIDATION
OF PROCESS COMMUNICATION

Gregor V. Bochmann
Département d'Informatique
et de Recherche Opérationnelle
Université de Montréal
Montreal, Canada

INTRODUCTION

Methods for the formal specification and logical validation of systems seem to
be of much greater practical importance for the design and implementation of
communication protocols than in the case of most other software products. This
is because the following typical difficulties arise in the design and implementation of communication protocols:

(a) Without a formal model, it is very difficult to foresee all possible modes
of operation that can occur due to varying synchronization between the communicating subsystems, possible malfunction of the communication medium,
and/or error recovery actions initiated by one or both subsystems.

(b) A protocol involves several interdependent parallel processes. In this
context, faults in the design and programming can give rise to time dependent errors which are very difficult to detect and locate by run time
tests. Therefore the logical validation of a protocol can be very useful
for detecting any design errors, thus complementing the usual testing
methods.

(c) Communication protocols must be implemented in a compatible way on all communicating subsystems. Often, the different subsystems are implemented on
different hardware, different operating systems, by different groups of
people, and in different organizations. Without a clear and non-ambiguous
protocol specification, this would be impossible.

This paper contains an introductory exposition of a protocol specification
method that involves finite state diagrams and programming variables for the
description of each of the communicating subsystems. Such a description can be
used as the basis for logical validation of the communication procedures. The
advantages of this method are shortly discussed.

VALIDATION METHODS

Traditionally, data communication protocols are specified in a kind of natural
language description which often leads to the problems of ambiguous meaning and
incompatible implementations. The need for more formal specification methods
has been realized, and different methods have been proposed for this purpose.
Such methods must not only provide a framework for a non-ambiguous and clear
definition of the protocol, but also facilitate the validation of the definition,
and lead to a correct implementation, usually in software.

A well-known method is the use of finite-state transition diagrams for the specification of the communicating subsystems (Bartlett et al. 1969; Merlin 1976).
The main advantage of this technique is the simplicity of the model, and the
possibility of using algorithms for deriving such properties as liveness of particular states or deadlock-freeness, which are useful for the validation of the

defined protocol. We showed that the communication medium used by the communicating subsystems can often be described by a finite state model as well (1976).
If one considers the medium as a resource which is shared between the communicating subsystems, one obtains a model which is much related to the description of
synchronization properties for shared resources by path expressions (Campbell
1974).

The main limitation of the finite state approach for protocol specification is,
again, its simplicity. For describing realistic protocols one usually needs a
very large number of states (which makes the description less readable), unless
one introduces hierarchical structuring of states and/or program variables, as
used by Bochmann and Chung (1977) for the description of HDLC procedures.
Another approach consists of describing each communicating subsystem in terms of
a process specified in a high-level programming language. In this case, no algorithms are available for the automatic validation of liveness and deadlock-
freeness, however, properties of the specified protocol can be verified by using
program assertions and invariants, as shown by Bochmann (1975) and Stenning
(1976).

COMBINING ASSERTIONS AND STATES

Validation of the interaction between two communicating subsystems usually
implies the verification of some global assertions, sometimes invariants,
involving the variables of both subsystems. However, in certain circumstances,
the global assertions involve not only the subsystem variables, but also the
process of execution in each subsystem. Such a situation occurs in particular
when each subsystem may execute recovery actions as considered by Randell (1975).

Two methods come to the mind for describing the process of execution in a subsystem: (1) the introduction of additional variables indicating the process of
execution of each subsystem, and (2) the use of a finite state program structure
with specified transitions from one state to another. We believe that the
second method leads often to a more readable description of communication protocols. Apart from readability, this approach presents the following advantages:

(a) The validation algorithms of the finite state approach mentioned
     above can be used for the finite state aspects of the communication
     protocol.

(b) Different assertions can be associated with the different states of a sub-
     system, and different global assertions can be associated with different
     pairs of states of the two subsystems.

(c) The combination of variables with the finite state approach and the associa-
     tion of executable statements with the transitions of a subsystem is an
     approach which integrates the complementary methods of finite-state des-
     cription and programming language description into a powerful and flexible
     model for the specification of interacting subsystems.

A particular formalism of this kind, related to the one of Keller (1976), is
proposed by Bochmann and Gecsei (1977) and has been successfully applied to the
description of a more complex protocol (Bochmann and Chung, 1977).

DISCUSSION

For the validation of interacting finite state subsystems one usually has to consider the product state space consisting of all pairs of states in subsystem 1
and 2, respectively (see for example Gilbert and Chandler (1972) or Merlin,
1976). It has been argued that this leads to a very large number of states to
be considered, the number of states in the product space being essentially equal
to n^2, where n is the number of states in each subsystem. We have however

noticed (1976) that in most practical examples the number of reachable pairs of states is much smaller because the nature of the communication medium restricts the possible transitions of the two subsystems.

Assertions that involve the process of execution of both subsystems cannot be associated with a given place in the program text of one subsystem, as is usually done for assertions involving only one process. However, they can be associated with a pair (or a set of pairs) of states in the product space. In the case that the assertion associated with all pairs is the same, it is called a "system invariant".

A simple inductive method for verifying the assertions Q_p associated with the state pairs p is as follows:

1°: Verify Q_{p_o} for the pair p_o of initial states.

2°: For each possible transition t of subsystem 1 or 2 respectively, leading from the state pair p to the pair p' , verify that

$$Q_p \wedge P_t \{S_t\} Q_{p'}$$

holds, where P_t is the enabling predicate of the transition t which must hold for the transition to be enabled, S_t is the statement executed during the transition t , which may change the values of the variables, and the notation $Q \{S\} Q'$ means that "Q holds immediately before the execution of statement S" implies that "Q' holds immediately after the execution of S".

REFERENCES

Bartlett, K.A., Scantlebury, R.A., and Wilkinson, P.T. (1969). A note on reliable full-duplex transmission over half-duplex links, CACM 12, 260.

Bochmann, G.V., and Chung, R.J. (1977). A formalized description of HDLC classes of procedures, to be presented at the Nat. Telecommunication Conf., Los Angeles, Dec. 1977.

Bochmann, G.V., and Gecsei, J. (1977). A unified method for the specification and verification of protocols, to be presented at IFIP Congress 1977, Toronto.

Bochmann, G.V. (1976). Finite State Description of Communication Protocols. Publication # 236, Dép. d'Informatique, Université de Montréal.

Bochmann, G.V. (1975). Logical verification and implementation of protocols, Proc. Fourth Data Communications Symposium (ACM/IEEE).

Brinch-Hansen, P. (1973). Operating Systems Principles, Englewood Cliffs, Prentice Hall.

Campbell, R.H. (1974). The specification of process synchronization by path expressions, in Colloque sur les Aspects Théoriques et Pratiques des Systèmes d'Exploitation, IRIA, Paris, pp. 93-106; and Campbell, R.H., and Habermann, A.N., idem, Technical Report No. 55, Computing Laboratory, Univ. of Newcastle upon Tyne.

Dijkstra, E.W. (1975). Guarded commands, non-determinacy and formal derivation of programs, CACM 18, p. 453-457.

Gilbert, P., and Chandler, W.J. (1972). Interference between communicating parallel processes, Comm. ACM 15, p. 427.

Keller, R.M. (1976). Formal Verification of Parallel Programs, CACM, 7, pp. 371-384.

Kotov, V.E. (1977). Concurrent programming with control types, in these proceedings.

Merlin, P.M. (1976). A methodology for the design and implementation of communication protocols, IEEE Transactions on Comm., Vol. COM-24, pp. 614-621.

Randell, B. (1975). System structure for software fault tolerance, Proc. Int.
  Conf. on Reliable Software, ACM Sigplan Notices Vol. 10, No. 6, p. 437.
Stenning, N.V. (1976). A data transfer protocol, Computer Networks, Vol. 1,
  No. 2, pp. 99-110.
Vaucher, J. (1973). A WAIT-UNTIL algorithm for general purpose simulation lan
  guages, Proc. Winter Simulation Conf., pp. 77-83, San Francisco.

ANNEX 3

Source: Canada

Title: Comments on formal description techniques

(Only parts of the paper are reproduced here)

3.   Defining a layer service

3.1 The service of a layer is provided through the upper layer interface. Different forms of interfaces (for the same service) may be
adopted in different parts of a distributed system. Therefore the
definition of the service should be, as much as possible, independent
of the particular interface through which it is provided.

3.2 A possible method for specifying a layer service is based on abstract
"service primitives". A service primitive is an element of the provided
service, making abstraction from the particular interface. A service
primitive may be invoked (i.e. its execution may be initiated) by
either side, service providing and using layers. It may provide for the
exchange of parameter values. For specifying a particular service, a
set of service primitives must be defined.

3.3 For certain considerations, it is not necessary to distinguish
whether the service primitive is initiated by the entity using the
service or the entity providing it. (For example, a "confirmed call
request" and an "accepted incoming call", in X.25, give rise to the
same connection). This should be supported by the notation for
service primitives (see for example Annex 1).

3.4 Usually, the service primitives that may be executed by a given
entity may not be executed in an arbitrary order and with arbitrary
parameter values. The permissible execution orders and parameter values
must be defined. This involves (a) local rules, and (b) global "end-to-
end" properties. The global properties are an essential part of the
communication service definition.

3.5 These considerations are illustrated by the example of Annex 1
which gives a possible definition of the link layer service. The
definition is structured into three parts:
(a)   list of service primitives (*Initialize, Terminate, Send, Receive*),
(b)   local rules,
(c)   global properties.
A local rule, for example, states that an entity using the service
must execute successfully the Initialize primitive before it may execute
a Send primitive for sending a data unit over the link. Global
properties, for example, state that the successful execution of a
Initialize primitive by one entity is always accompained by a simultaneous
execution of such a primitive by the peer entity, and that the next
Receive primitive executed by the latter delivers the same data unit
which was provided as parameter for the execution of the Send primitive
by the former.

Annex 1: Service provided by an HDLC protocol (example of a link layer service)

1. List of service primitives (at the layer interface of a given station)

↓ Init: Initialize primitive initiated by the entity using the service (in layer above)

↑ Init: Initialize primitive initiated by the HDLC station (entity of the link layer)

↓ uns. Init: Unsuccessful Initialize primitive

↑ Term : Termination initiated by ...

↓ Term : Termination initiated by ...

↓ Send (data): primitive for sending a service data unit

↑ Receive (data): primitive for receiving a service data unit

Status functions

- circuit-inoperable : true..false (becomes true after "too many" retransmissions)

- outstanding : 0..7

- not-yet-sent : integer

Notes: (a) The arrows "↓" and "↑" indicate which layer initiates the primitive, i.e. the entity below or above the service interface, respectively. "↕" means "↑" or "↓"

(b) The status functions do not influence the operation.

2. Local rules for using the primitives

The possible orders of execution for these primitives at a given station are defined by the transition diagram below. The data parameter of the Send or Receive primitives is arbitrary, provided its length is not too long ($\leq \ell$ max). The status functions may be called any time (between the execution of primitives).

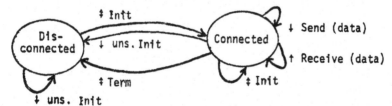

↓ uns. Init

Note: This diagram represents an abstraction of the operation of the HDLC protocol at the given station (operation of the link layer protocol), as described in Annex 2.

3. Global properties of the service primitives

(a) For each (successful) Initialize primitive executed at the end of the link where it is initiated, there is at least one execution of such a primitive at the same time at the other end. (This is not in general true for the Terminate primitive; for example, in the case of a circuit failure, the entity using the service at the primary station may execute the Terminate primitive without the secondary noticing).

(b) The sequence of data parameters passed by the Receive primitives between two consecutive Initialize executions is identical to the sequence of the first data parameters passed by the Send primitives at the opposite end of the link between two corresponding Initialize executions.

(c) Refering to (b) above, if n_r and n_s are the numbers of Receive and Send executions, respectively, then $(n_s - n_r)$ is $\geqslant 0$, and lies between not-yet-sent and (not-yet-sent + outstanding). (I.e. $(n_s - n_r)$ data units are lost).

ANNEX   4

A FORMALIZED SPECIFICATION OF HDLC CLASSES OF PROCEDURES*

Gregor V. Bochmann and Richard J. Chung
Département d'informatique et de recherche opérationnelle
Université de Montréal
Montréal, Canada

The paper is concerned with the problem of clearly specifying, validating and implementing communication procotols. A unified model for protocol specification is used which combines finite state transition diagrams with program variables and statements. The paper presents a formalized specification of some standard HDLC classes of procedures for controlling data transmission over synchronous circuits. This example was chosen because (a) it is of general interest, and (b) the available descriptions in natural language are complex enough such that the validation of operational characteristics, and a correct implementation of these protocols are difficult to obtain.

Before presenting the detailed specification of the protocols, the paper explains the description formalism used. Some new structuring concepts are introduced which allow the decomposition of the protocol specification into several relatively independent components. This reduces the complexity of the protocol description and thus facilitates the understanding, validation and implementation of the defined protocols.

1. Introduction

Data communication is an area joining the traditionally distinct disciplines of communication technology and data processing. In particular, most communication protocols used in data and computer networks are implemented in software on host, front-end or special purpose communication computers. This paper is concerned with the problems of clearly specifying, validating and implementing communication protocols. We believe that a formalized description method can be very useful for obtaining a clear and non-ambiguous protocol specification, and also be useful ·for validating and implementing the protocol in question[1].

In this paper, we present a formalized specification of some HDLC classes of procedures [2,3,4] to be used for controlling data transmission between several stations over a point-to-point or multi-point synchronous circuit. We have chosen this example because (a) it is of general interest and (b) the available descriptions in natural language are complex enough such that the validation of operational characteristics, and a correct implementation of these protocols are difficult to obtain. We hope that the specification given in this paper may be useful for these purposes. Similarly as the above mentioned standard specifications, our description of the HDLC procedures leaves many details unspecified. These details must be determined for each particular implementation. The reason for leaving these details unspecified is that they are not relevant for validating the operation of the protocols and for obtaining compatibility between the different implementations.

Section 2 of this paper gives a short introduction to the formalism used for the description of the HDLC procedures. Essentially, it is a combination of a high-level programming language and finite state diagrams[5]. We also use the concept of abstract data types[6] for describing the different components of a station. Certain aspects of the formalism, such as the coupling of transitions, are new or have never been used for this purpose.

Section 3 and the annex contain a formalized specification of the unbalanced classes of HDLC procedures and some necessary explanations. Sections 4 and 5 give some comments on a possible approach to the implementation of the procedures, and on the validation of operational characteristics.

2. Description Formalism

The formalism used in this paper for the description of the HDLC procedures is based on the unified model of Bochmann and Gecsei[5] and uses some additional concepts.

2.1. Finite state transition diagrams

We use finite state transition diagrams consisting of a set of places connected by directed arcs, called transitions. Each transition is characterized by an enabling predicate and an action, specified in terms of a high-level programming language, such as Pascal and program variables. A transition may fire only when the originating place contains a token and the enabling predicate is true. The firing of a transition consists of the transfer of the token to the destination place, and the execution of the action, as specified for the transition. At any given time, at most one transition is being fired at a given station (except in the case of direct coupling, as explained below).

For example, the transition diagram of the *source* component of an HDLC station (see annex 6.) has two states and several transitions. The transition RR leading (from either state) to the *Remote Ready* state is enabled (see table of transitions) when the station variable *received.kind* has the value RR. (As in Pascal, the notation *received.kind* means the element *kind* of the composite data structure *received*). The action executed by the RR transition (see table of transitions) consists of three statements, the execution of the *examine-NR* procedure, the *checkpointing* procedure if the received P/F bit is one, and the reinitialization of the *transmission* component for being ready to receive the next frame.

2.2 Distantly initiated actions

We consider that the overall system consists of several stations (called "subsystems" in ref. 5) located at different points in space. Each station, independently of each other, is described by program variables and state transitions. For simplifying the description of a station, the variables and transitions are grouped into several functional components, (see for example the overview in the annex). A component consists of program variables of simple or abstract data types

* This work was supported in part by the National Research Council of Canada and the Ministère de l'Education du Québec.

see section 2.6) and may be associated with a transition diagram. The operation of different components f a given station is interrelated as explained in subsections 2.3 through 2.5.

For describing the interrelation between different stations, we use the concept of distantly initiated actions[5]. These actions are not associated with transitions, but are executed at a given station some finite time after they have been initiated (by an INITIATE statement) by a different (distant) station.

As shown in annex 3, this mecanism can be used for describing the synchronous circuit and HDLC frame structure[8] used as communication medium by the HDLC procedures. The (distantly initiated) action *transmit* of the HDLC station is, for instance, initiated by the execution, at a distant station, of the procedure *send-supervisory*. The execution of the *transmit* action corresponds to the reception of a frame. If the frame is correctly received and is a RR-kind of frame (this information has been passed as a parameter by the distant station during initiation) then the *received.kind* will set to the value RR, and the RR transition of the source component can subsequently be fired, as explained above.

3 Parallel independent components

Unless hierarchical dependence or direct coupling (see below) is specified for the interrelation between different station components, their interrelation is characterized as follows. The state of each component is determined by the values of the variables and the currently active place of the transition diagram, indicated by the presence of a token. The tokens of the different components make transitions independently of one another, in any order, but the transitions exclude one another in time, so that mutual exclusion is enforced for access to shared variables. The only interrelation between the components comes from the fact that the actions associated with the transitions of a given component can change the values of variables of the same or other components, and the enabling predicates of the transitions, in turn, may depend on these variables.

4 Hierarchically dependent components

Each component can be set to its initial state by the execution of an *init* statement. We consider a component X to be hierarchically dependent on a component Y if X is initialized whenever Y enters a particular state, which we call the activating state for X, and X is passivated whenever Y leaves this state.

As an example, we mention the two parallel components *source* and *sink* of the HDLC station that, are hierarchically dependent on the *link-set-up* component, where the activating state for the *source* and the *sink* is the *Connected* state. When the *link-set-up* component is in the *Connected* state the transitions of the components *source* and *sink* proceed independently of one other, as explained above, until the *link-set-up* component fires a transition at which instant the *sink* and *source* components are passivated. They are reactivated and reinitialized when the *link-set-up* component enters the *Connected* state again.

This concept has also been used in the description of the packet level procedures of the X.25 network access protocol[9], and a similar approach has been used by Bjorner[10]. The concept is useful for expressing hierarchical structure and abstraction in the top-down design of systems.

2.5 Direct coupling between transitions of different components

The concept of direct coupling introduces a strong synchronization between the transitions of different components. The idea of direct coupling consists of requiring that with certain transitions of one component, there must be certain "directly coupled" transitions of another component that fire simultaneously[11]. Such a transition can only fire when itself is enabled and one of its directly coupled transitions is also enabled.

In the case of the HDLC station, such a direct coupling is established between the underlined transitions of the *link-set-up*, *source* and *sink* components on the one hand, and the underlined transitions of the *PF-control* component on the other hand, which correspond to the frame sending transition of the station. For example, a NRM secondary station (see annex 8.2) with a token in the *Polled* state of the *PF-control* component can send an <u>CMDR</u>, I, <u>RR</u>, <u>RNR</u> or <u>REJ</u> frame (depending on the state of the *link-set-up*, *source* or *sink* component), with a F-bit equal to zero or one (transition F_0 or F_1 respectively). Similarly, a primary station with a token in the *Polling* state of the *PF-control* component and a token in the *Wait-for-SXRM-ack* state of the *link-set-up* component (see annex 8.1 and 5.1) has to wait until the *clock* component enables the $P_{1-retrans}$ transition (enabling predicate is *status = time-out*) before it could retransmit a SXRM frame. A similar coupling is established between the corresponding non-underlined (receiving) transitions.

We note that the concepts of hierarchical dependence and direct coupling are introduced here as pragmatic tools for managing the complexity of the described protocols in a comprehensive way. These concepts represent extension to the unified model described in ref. 5, but they do not provide any additional power. There are simple schemes for transforming a given system specification using the concepts outlined in this section into an equivalent specification using the unified model.

2.6 Abstract data types

The concept of abstract data types has been proposed for specifying the properties of a program module independently of the details of its operation. This allows changing the implementation of the operation without affecting the interface of the module with other system components.

We illustrate this concept with the following example: the *sink* component contains a local *buffer* variable which is used to deliver received data to the user process. Instead of specifying how this buffer is to be implemented, we only describe the interface of this buffer with the *sink* component. This interface consists of the function *space* and the procedure *put*. (The interface of the buffer with the user process is ignored in this description). Only the properties of the interface are specified, but not the details of how the *put* procedure, for instance, is executed. These details are left to be determined by the implementation which must satisfy the properties of the interface. Only the latter are relevant for the validation of the protocol. A more elaborate discussion of abstract data types can be found elsewhere[6].

3. Description of HDLC procedures

The HDLC procedures defined in this paper follow
closely the standard specifications [2,3,4]. The procedures for link set up and clearing are given only for unbalanced classes of procedures; the procedures for
data transfer apply to unbalanced and balanced classes.
We hope, but do not guarantee that the procedures follow in all aspects the standard specifications; however, they are in some aspects more specific than the
ISO standard[2]. For example, our description specifies
a P-bit equal to one for link-set-up and clearing commands. This has the effect that the time-out recovery
mecanism provided by the *PF-control* component is not
only used in the data transfer phase, but also in the
link-set-up and clearing phase. We hope that the choices we made represent a reasonable interpretation of
the standard.

We consider a station that communicates according
to an HDLC procedure with other stations connected
through a synchronous circuit. A station consists of
a number of components, as shown in annex 1. Not all
of these components are present in each station, and
several of the components exist in different versions.
Which components are present in a given station and
which versions are chosen depend on the type of station
and configuration in which it is used. In unbalanced
configurations one distinguishes between primary stations (responsible for link-set-up, clearing and link
error recovery) and secondary stations, between half-
duplex and full-duplex transmission, and between NRM
(i.e. normal response mode in which the secondary station only sends frames to the primary after being polled by the latter) and ARM (i.e. asynchronous response
mode in which the secondary may send frames any time).

For multi-point configurations, one uses one primary station and several secondary stations, usually
in NRM. Each frame sent over the transmission link contains an address field (also present in point-to-point
configurations) which indicates the address of the
relevant secondary station. The primary station contains one set of functional components (see overview,
annex1)for each secondary station it serves. We call
such a set a sub-station. Each sub-station of the
primary is responsible for the communication with one
secondary station. Each secondary station contains
only   one sub-station. The multiplexing of several
sub-stations within one primary station is not described here, since it is considered a detail of implementation.

The operation of an HDLC sub-station is specified
in the annex. Annex 1 gives an overview of the different components that can occur in a sub-station. The
components that are present in each sub-station are the
transmission, link-set-up and *Pf-control* components,
the other components are present as needed. The annex
shows for each component, if appropriate,the transition
diagram and a table containing the enabling predicates
and actions of the transitions, the relevant program
variables, the initial state, and possibly some action
procedures. We do not give more explanations here since we hope that the protocol description is self-expla-
natory. Nevertheless, the references given above may
be helpful for a better understanding.

4. Implementation

4.1 Choices left to the implementation

As already mentioned, the protocol specifications
in the annex leave many details to be chosen by the implementation. Among these choices we mention the following most important issues:

(a) Choice of transition: In many occasions, several

different transitions are enabled according to the
specifications given. The implementation may
choose among these transitions any one for firing
(execution), depending on the requirements of the
application.

(b) Choice of the P/F bit: The frequency of polling
and/or check-pointing as determined by the *PF-control* is left to the discretion of the implementer.

(c) The determination of the order and priority of
service for the different secondary stations in a
multi-point configuration is left to the implementation.

(d) The detailed form of the interface between the
user processes (i.e. application) and the communication protocol is implementation dependent.

We note, by the way, that an implementation of
the described HDLC procedures may very well inquire, in
addition to the application requirements, the detailed
state of the different station components. This information may be used for determining the next action to
be taken whenever several choices are possible, particularly during error recovery.

4.2 Programming tools for implementation

Compared to a protocol specification written in
natural language, the specification given in the annex
is relatively easy to implement, since it is already
written in terms of a programming language. The main
difficulties lie in the realization of the implementation choices outlined above, and in the parallel proce-
sing nature of the sending and receiving operations of
the protocol and the application processes. For the
latter point, a programming language allowing the specification of several parallel processes seems advan-
tageous. Facilities for programming with abstract data
structures are also very useful. High level programming
languages that provide these facilities are being designed and can already be used for the implementation of
communication protocols such as those described in this
paper.

5. Validation

Based on the specification of the HDLC procedures
given in the annex, validation could be obtained through
two complementary approaches[5]:

(1) an analysis of the reachable states of the communicating stations, taking into account only the
finite state structure of the transition diagram
of the two stations;

(2) establishment of assertions about the values of
program variables, associated with certain states
of the stations.

Both approaches are interrelated since the values of
the program variables determine partly which transition
are enabled. We note that the component structure of
the protocol description will facilitate the verification of different protocol properties independently of
one another.

We consider the following operational characteristics of the protocol as interesting candidates for
verification:

(a) Synchronization between primary and secondary stations for link set-up, resetting and clearing in
the presence of transmission errors, lost frames
and command rejection conditions.

(b) Correct data transmission in the connected
state in the presence of transmission errors and
lost frames.

(c) Effectiveness of the flow control mechanism.

(d) Possibilities of data loss during link resetting
and clearing.

(e) Absence of deadlocks and undesired loops.

6. Conclusions

We hope that the formalized specification of the
HDLC classes of procedures given in the annex may be
useful for a better understanding of their operation,
for their validation, and for obtaining correct implementations. (The specification is presently being
used for an implementation of the X.25 link access
procedures[9]). We beleive that such a formalized specification would be a good format for the official
definition of a protocol, in this case of the HDLC
procedures, since it is more concise and less ambiguous than a specification in natural language.
However, it should be complemented by an informal text
in natural language providing necessary explanations
of the background, the scope of application, and comments on the operation of the procedures.

Acknowledgements

We would like to thank Jan Gecsei for many interesting discussion and suggestions. We also thank Mr.
O.B.P. Rikkert de Koe for useful comments and for
bringing the timer state diagrams of ref. 4 to our at-
tention.

7. References

1. G.V. Bochmann, "Logical verification and implementation of protocols", Proc. Fourth Data Communications Symposium (ACM/IEEE, 1975), p. 7.15-7.20.
2. Data Communication - HDLC - Elements of procedures,
Draft International Standard ISO/DIS 4335 (1976).
3. HDLC Proposed Unbalanced Classes of Procedures,
ISO/TC 97/SC 6/N 1339 (1976).
4. HDLC classes of procedure, ECMA Working Paper,
TC 9/76/55 (1976).
5. G.V. Bochmann and J. Gecsei, "A unified method for
the specification and verification of protocols"
in Proceedings IFIP Congress 1977, Toronto, p. 229.
6. B.H. Liskov and S.N. Zilles, "Specification techniques for data abstractions", IEEE Trans. on Software Engineering, SE-1, p.7 (1975).
7. K. Jensen and N. Wirth, "Pascal User Manual and
Report", Springer Verlag, Berlin, 1974.
8. ISO 3309, Data communication - HDLC - Frame Structure.
9. CCITT, Recommendation X.25 (1976).
10. D. Bjorner, "Finite state automation - definition
of data communication line control procedures",
Proceedings FJCC 1970, p. 477.
11. G.V. Bochmann, "Finite state description of communication protocols", Publication # 236, Dép.
d'Informatique, Université de Montréal, 1976.

ANNEX: OPERATION OF AN HDLC SUB-STATION

A sub-station consists of several functional components, as shown in section 1. Each sub-station contains at least a *link-set-up*, *PF-control* and *transmission* component, and other components as needed. The detailed operation of the components is specified by the tables and transition diagrams below. We note that the underlined transitions are frame sending transitions, whereas the non-underlined transitions correspond (in general) to the reception of a frame.

The *source* and *sink* components, if present, are hierarchically dependent on the *link-set-up* component, where *Connected* is the activating state, i.e. the *source* and *sink* components are initialized whenever the *link-set-up* component enters the *Connected* state, and are passivated when the *Connected* state is left.

The *PF-control* component is directly coupled with the other components such that an underlined (non-underlined) transition of the *PF-control* component is always fired simultaneously with an underlined (non-underlined) transition of the *link-set-up*, *source* or *sink* component.

1. OVERVIEW OF THE COMPONENTS OF AN HDLC STATION

Link-set-up component

Transitions: SXRM, DISC, UA, CMDR, ERROR (primary) and SXRM, DISC, UA, CMDR (secondary).

Versions: -Primary station: see section 5.1
-Secondary station: see section 5.2
-Balanced station : not included here

Source component

Transitions: I, RNR, RR, REJ

Variables: buffer, VS, unack

For details: see section 6

Sink component

Transitions: I, RNR, RR, REJ

Variables: buffer, VR

Versions: -Sink without Reject: see section 7.1
-Sink with REJ: see section 7.2
-Sink with SREF: not included here

PF-control component

Transitions: P_0, P_1, F_0, F_1, $P_{1\text{-retrans}}$ (primary) and P_0 P_1, F_0, F_1, (secondary)

Variable : bit

Versions: -Primary in NRM:⎫
-Primary in ARM:⎭ see section 8.1
-Secondary in NRM:⎫
-Secondary in ARM:⎭ see section 8.2

Clock component

Transition: TICK

Variables: timer

For details: see section 9

Transmission component

No transitions: procedures are called by other components.

Variables: received, status

Distantly initiated action: transmit

For details: see section 3

Checkpoint component

No transitions: procedures are called by other components

Variables: VS, inhibit (depending on type of station)

Several versions: for details see section 4

2. DATA TYPES AND CONSTANTS

Constants	Meaning
modulus = 8;	modulus of sequence numbers for I-frames

Types

info-type = ... ;	for information field of a frame
address-type = ... ;	for addresses assigned to secondary stations
sequence-count = 0 .. modulus -1 ;	
frame-kind = (none, I, RR, RNR, REJ, SARM, SNRM, DISC, UA, CMDR) ;	

control-type = record
  kind : frame-kind ;
  pfbit: (0 .. 1) ;
  NS : sequence-count ;
  NR : sequence-count
  end ;
	elements within the control field of HDLC frame structure

frame-type = record
  address : address-type ;
  control-field ; control-type ;
  info : info-type ;
  end ;
	elements within an HDLC frame structure

status-type = set of
  [invalid-control-field,
  invalid-info,
  invalid-size,
  invalid-NR,
  time-out] ;
	for error reporting by secondary

TRANSMISSION COMPONENT

Variables	Meaning
received : frame-type ;	frame received as a result of the execution of a distantly initiated *transmit* action
status : status-type ;	status of frame received or timeout condition

Initial State

status =[ ] ;	normal status
received. kind = none ;	

Procedures (called by other components)

examine-NR ;

{This procedure releases the buffers and updates the source variables according to received.NR }

begin
  if received. NR ≠ source.unack
  then begin source.buffer.free-until (received.NR) ;
              source.unack := received.NR ;
       end
end ;

validate (received:frame-type; status : status-type);

{This procedure validates the address, control and info fields of the received frame and sets the status accordingly. If the status is not normal (*status ≠* [ ]) then the *received.kind* will be set to *none*. In particular it checks that *received.NR* lies between *source.unack* and *source.VS*.}

The following send procedures prepare the appropriate frame for transmission by taking the address of the active sub-station and the P/F-bit from the PF-control function which is executed. The frame is formated and transmitted according to the HDLC frame structure[8].

send-info (VS,VR : sequence-count; info-to-send : info-type) ;

begin
  INITIATE (transmit,frame) where
    frame.address := ... ,
    frame.kind   := I ,
    frame.pfbit   := PF-control.bit ,
    frame.NS   := VS ,
    frame.NR   := VR ,
    frame.info   := info-to-send
end ;

send-supervisory (send-kind : (RR, RNR, REJ);
  VR:sequence-count) {similar}

send-unnumbered (send-kind : (SNRM, SARM, DISC, UA));
  {similar}

send-CMDR (control-field : control-type;
  VS,VR: sequence-count ; status : status-type) ;
  { similar}

Distantly initiated action	Meaning:
transmit (frame) ;	depending on the transmission medium one of the following will occur
begin	
case reception of	
loss : ;	message loss
FCSerror : ;	transmission error, frame ignored.
CorrectFCS : begin	
received := frame ;	frame correctly received: the frame is validated and passed to the appropriate sub-station
validate (received, status)	
end	
end ;	

4. CHECKPOINT COMPONENT

Variables	Meaning:
VS : sequence-count	value of VS when P or F = 1 is sent (used for full duplex transmission only).
inhibit : boolean	set to false when P or F = 1 is sent, and to true when REJ is received with P or F = 0

Procedures (called by other components)

setcheckpoint ; {This procedure remembers the value of VS when a P/F cycle is started, i.e. a P/F bit = 1 is sent}
begin
  checkpoint.VS:= source.VS ;
  inhibit:= false
end ;

checkpointing ; {This procedure may induce retransmission of I-frames according to P/F bit error recovery}
begin
  if not inhibit and
    (received.NR - source.unack) mod modulus ≤
    (checkpoint.VS - source.unack) mod modulus
    {not all I-frames sent when the P-bit was sent have been acknowledged (when the F-bit is received)}
  then source.VS := received. NR ; {retransit}

end ;

Note: The procedures can be simplified in certain cases:

(a) In the case of a FDX primary or an ARM secondary, the procedures above must be used.

(b) In the case of a NRM secondary or HDX primary, no action is needed for *setcheckpoint*, and the action of *checkpointing* could be simply
source.VS := received.VR.

(c) In the case that REJ is not used, the value of *inhibit* is always false.

5. LINK-SET-UP COMPONENT

Transition diagrams

5.1 Primary Station   **5.2 Secondary Station**

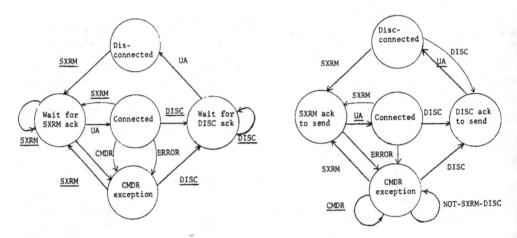

Initial   state: token in *Disconnected*

Transition	Enabling predicate	Action	Meaning
Primary station:			
SXRM	PF-control.bit = 1	send-unnumbered (SXRM) ;	SXRM is SNRM or SARM dependi on the mode to be set
UA	received.kind = UA	init (source) ; init (sink) ; init (transmission) ;	initialize the source and si components
DISC	PF-control.bit = 1	send-unnumbered (DISC);	
CMDR	received.kind = CMDR	init (transmission) ;	

ERROR	Status in
	[invalid-control-field,
	  invalid-info,
	  invalid-size,
	  invalid-NR]
		init (transmission) ;	frame received contained an ror to be resolved by a high level recovery procedure at Primary

OTHER	...	init (transmission) ;	in certain states, the recep tion of certain kinds of fra is simply ignored (not shown the transition diagram).
Secondary station:			
SXRM	received.kind = SXRM	init (transmission) ;	SXRM is SNRM or SARM dependi on the mode set
UA	PF-control.bit = 1	send-unnumbered (UA) ;	
DISC	received.kind = DISC	init (transmission) ;	
CMDR	true	send-CMDR (received.control-field, source.VS, sink.VR, status);	report procedural error for recovery by primary
ERROR (as above)			
NOT SXRM DISC	not (received.kind in [SNRM, SARM, DISC])	init (transmission) ;	

6. SOURCE COMPONENT

<u>Transition diagram</u>

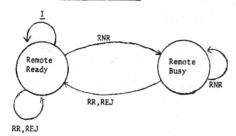

<u>Initial State</u>

Token in *Remote Ready* ;
VS = 0 ;
unack = 0 ;

riables	Meaning
ack : sequence-count ;	oldest frame sent in sequence but not yet acknowledged
: sequence-count ;	next frame to be sent
ffer	
data(VS : sequence-count);	function which returns the buffer of data to be sent.
to-send (VS : sequence-count) ;	boolean function which is true when there is a buffer of data to be sent.
free-until (NR : sequence-count) ;	procedure to release buffers of data that have been acknowledged.

ansition	Enabling predicate	Action	Meaning

I	buffer.to-send (VS)
	
	VS ≠ (unack + window) mod modulus
		if PF-control.bit = 1 then
		   setcheckpoint;
		send-info (VS,sink.VR,
		   buffer.data (VS)) ;
		VS := (VS+1) mod modulus ;
			when there is an I frame to be sent, which lies within the send window, send it

RNR	received.kind = RNR	examine-NR ; if received.pfbit=1 then checkpointing ; init (transmission) ;	
RR	received.kind = RR	... idem ...	

REJ	received.kind = REJ	examine-NR;
		if received.pfbit = 0 then
		   checkpoint.inhibit = true;
		VS := received.NR ;
		init (transmission);
			rejection recovery should inhi-bit P/F checkpointing
			
			induces retransmission

te: According to this specification the *remote busy* condition is cleared only on the reception of a RR or REJ frame (see also ref. 2).

7. SINK COMPONENT

Transition diagrams

7.1 Sink without Reject   **7.2 Sink with REJ**

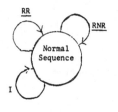

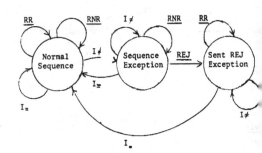

Variables	Meaning
VR : sequence-count	sequence number of next I-frame which will be accepted
buffer	
space	boolean function which returns the value true when there is a buffer availab⌐ for receiving data
put(data:info-type)	procedure for delivering data to the user.

Initial State

Token in *Normal Sequence* ;
$VR = 0$;

Transition	Enabling predicate	Action	Meaning
I	received.kind = I	examine-NR ; if received.pfbit=1 then checkpointing ; if received.NS≠VR then forward-data ; init (transmission)	if I-frame is in sequence, pass data to user (if ready)
RR	buffer.space	if PF-control.bit = 1 then setcheckpoint; send-supervisory (RR, source.VS, VR) ;	
RNR	¬buffer.space	if PF-control.bit = 1 then setcheckpoint; send-supervisory (RNR, source.VS, VR) ;	
REJ	buffer.space {REJ clears busy }	if PF-control.bit = 1 then setcheckpoint; send-supervisory (REJ, source.VS, VR) ;	
I≠	received.kind = I ∧ received.NS ≠ VR	examine-NR ; if received.pfbit = 1 then checkpointing; init (transmission) ;	info field is ignored
I=	received.kind = I ∧ received.NS = VR	... idem ... forward-data ;	pass data to user (if ready)

Procedure

forward-data ; {This procedure passes the data received to the user and updates the next expected sequence
        number.}
           begin
              if buffer.space
              then begin buffer.put(received.data) ; VR := (VR+1) mod modulus end
            end ;

8. PF-CONTROL COMPONENT
8.1 Primary station
Transition diagrams

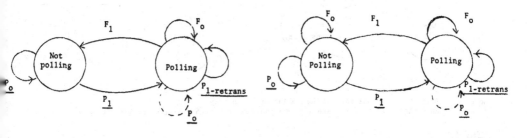

Normal response mode (NRM)   Asynchronous response mode (ARM)

Note: Dotted transitions in full duplex transmission only.

Variables	Meaning
bit : 0 .. 1 ;	P/F bit ; the value is set dynamically by the implementation of the higher level

Initial State

taken in *Not polling*

Transition	Enabling predicate	Action	Meaning
P_0	bit = 0		
P_1	bit = 1	timer := t_0 ;	start timer
$P_{1-retrans}$	status=[timeout] $\wedge$ bit = 1	... idem ...	
F_0	received.pfbit = 0	if timer > 0 then timer := t_0 ;	if timer is running, restart it (according to ref. 2 not for FDX)
F_1	received.pfbit = 1	timer := 0 ;	stop timer

8.2 Secondary station

Transition diagrams

Normal response mode (NRM)

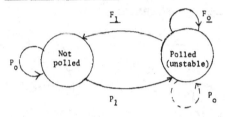

Asynchronons response mode (ARM)

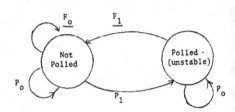

Note: (1) Dotted transitions in full duplex transmission only
(2) An unstable state rust make a sending transition at the earliest opportunity.

Variables	Meaning
bit : 0 .. 1 ;	P/F bit ; value is set dynamically by the implementation of the higher level

Initial State

Token in *Not polled*

Transition	Enabling predicate	Action
P_0	received.pfbit = 0	
P_1	received.pfbit = 1	
F_0	bit = 0	
F_1	bit = 1	

9. CLOCK COMPONENT

Transition diagram

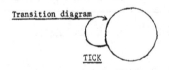

TICK

Variable
    timer : integer {time counter}
Initial State
    Token in the place

Transition	Enabling predicate	Action
TICK	true	timer := timer - 1 ; if timer = 0 then status := [timeout] ;

ANNEX 5

DEVELOPMENT AND STRUCTURE OF AN X.25 IMPLEMENTATION

by

Gregor V. Bochmann and Tankoano Joachim

April 1978

ABSTRACT

The paper describes experience with an implementation of the X.25 communication protocols for accessing public data networks. The implementation effort is characterized by (a) the development of a formalized protocol specification on which all further implementation work is based, and (b) by the use of Concurrent Pascal as the implementation language. The main features of the formalized protocol specification are given, and a method for deriving a protocol implementation based on parallel processes, *monitors* and *classes* is explained. The overall structure of the system, and the step-wise refinements leading to the complete implementation are discussed. Some comments on the possible implementation on multiple microprocessors are also given.

1. INTRODUCTION

X.25 [1] is a standard access protocol for using virtual circuits (VC's) provided by public data networks. This paper describes certain aspects of the experience gained from the implementation of this protocol in a host computer [2] . For the implementation of most communication protocols the following points must be considered :

(a) ensuring the compatibility of the implementation with the remote communication partner,

(b) implementing several parallel activities, which is usual for real-time systems, and

(c) a step-wise refinement of the system design, which is a useful discipline for any software development project.

We have used a high-level implementation language [3] which provides the concepts of abstract data types (i.e. *class*), parallel processes, and *monitors* (for process interaction). These concepts support the points (b) and (c) above. In view of point (a), we have used a formalized specification of the X.25 protocol. Part of our project was the development of this specification. More precise and more algorithmical in nature than the original specification of the protocol, given in natural language, it has been used as the basis for deriving the implementation in a more or less straightforward manner, as described in section 3.

Section 2 describes the main features of the formalized X.25 specification as used in our project. (The complete specification is contained in [2]). Section 3 explains how such a formalized specification may be transformed into an implementation, taking one component of the X.25 link level as an example. In section 4, we describe the overall structure of our X.25 implementation as far as the organization of parallel activity is concerned, and the interfaces between the different system parts, including the user of the VC communication facility provided. In section 5, we make some remarks on the step-wise refinement of our system and discuss in some detail the problems of buffer management and message coding. We finish with some general conclusions from our implementation experience. The complete text of our formalized specification of X.25, and its implementation in Concurrent Pascal is contained in [2].

We assume in the following some familiarity with the X.25 protocol [1], the concepts of classes, processes and monitors as realized in Concurrent Pascal [3], and the unified protocol specification method of Bochmann and Gecsei [4].

2. A FORMALIZED SPECIFICATION OF X.25

The X.25 specification contains three procedure layers :

(1) the physical layer, specifying bit transmission between the subscriber and network equipments,

(2) the link layer, specifying frame formats, transmission error detection, and error recovery procedures, and

(3) the packet layer, specifying packet formats and procedures for the use of VC's.

A basic decomposition of the X.25 protocol is shown in figure 1, where the different modules communicate by exchanging packets or frames, respectively. The *VC control* modules implement the packet level procedures, separately for each VC, and the *Packet sender* and *receiver* modules implement the link level procedures. These procedures have been considered for the formalized specification. The other modules of figure 1 have essentially a (de-) multiplexing function, and are relatively simple. The *Frame input* and *output* modules also handle transmission error detection and transparency coding, as well as physical input/output. We note that the X.25 link level (we consider the original LAP A standard [1]) distinguishes primary and secondary functions which, relatively independent of one another, perform the sending and receiving of frames, respectively. This is reflected by separate *Packet sender* and *receiver* modules.

2.1 The link layer

The link level procedures describe a particular class of HDLC procedures. A formalized specification of HDLC procedures, in general, has been described elsewhere [5]. Our formalized specification of the X.25 link level is based, as far as possible, on that specification, and therefore uses the same specification formalism.

The HDLC procedures may be considered [5] to be composed out of several different, interrelated components, as shown in figure 2. The link between the computer and the network is set up (and disconnected) separately for each direction of frame transmission, by the *Link set-up* components. The *Source* and *Sink* components perform the frame transmission during the *connected* state; and the *PF control* components determine the exchange of poll/final (PF) bits [1]. The *Clock* component provides a time-out mecanism for retransmission.

In the formalized specification, each component is characterized by program variables, a transition diagram and enabling predicates and actions for each transition. All transitions exclude one another in time, and a given transition may only be executed when its enabling predicate, which depends on the variables, is true. When executed, the transition action may update the variables and thus enable or disable other transitions of the same and other components (for more detail, see [4]). As an example we show in Figure 3 the specification of the *Primary link set-up* component. The transition diagram of figure 3(a) shows the possible transitions. Figure 3(c) shows, for each transition, when it may be executed and what its action is. Enabling predicates, as well as actions may involve variables of other components, which are written in the form "<component name >.<variable name >". The local variables of the *Link set-up* component are listed in figure 3(b).

There are certain differences between our formalized specification of the X.25 link level procedures and the specification of HDLC given in [5] . They may be attributed to the following two factors:

(a) The X.25 procedures operate in a particular configuration including a primary and a secondary station, and in asynchronous response mode only.

(b) One objective of the specifications in [5] was to include only those aspects that are necessary to ensure the compatibility between the communicating system parts. For the X.25 specification we have included additional aspects, not essential for compatibility. These aspects include points described in the standard, points adopted for the subscriber equipment by analogy with the specifications for the network equipment, and an interface to a higher level link manager module.

A comparison between the two formalized specifications may be made comparing figures 3(d) and (c). Finally, figure 3(e) shows some pieces of text describing the use of the SARM command (one of the topics relevant to this component) extracted from the standard specification [1] .

2.2 *The packet layer*

We found that the same specification techniques used for the link layer could be easily applied to the description of the packet level procedures. We adopted the decomposition of the layer into the components shown in figure 4, with a hierarchical dependence [5] between the different components. The *restart* component is the hierarchically highest component on which all VC's depend; the components of only one VC are shown. A timer component seems to be necessary for a realistic system, although this aspect has been ignored in the standard.

As in the case of the link layer, each component is described by variables, transition diagrams and transitions. Most of the transition diagrams given in the annex of the standard have been adapted, and completed with an *error* state and corresponding transitions. As an example, we show the transition diagram of the *Reset* component in figure 5.

3.   IMPLEMENTATION TRANSFORMATIONS

We now explain how the formalized protocol specification discussed above may be transformed into an implementation in terms of processes, monitors, and classes. As mentioned above, a system component is characterized by

variables, a transition diagram, and enabling predicates and actions for
each transition. A straightforward realization of a component could be obtained
using conditional critical regions, for which an efficient implementation,
however, is not always easy to obtain [6]. We have chosen an implementation
pattern where a component is generally implemented by a monitor and some
processes. The monitor contains the component variables, a variable representing
the state of the transition diagram, and procedures which, when called, effect
the component transitions. The processes represent different external events
and call these procedures. The transition of the *Primary link set-up* component,
for example, are activated by two processes representing the reception and
sending of frames over the network access circuit, as shown in figure 6.

This implementation approach works for independent components, such
as the *Primary* and *Secondary link set-up* components of the X.25 link layer. In
the case of component dependences, we have adopted the following implementation
patterns:

(a) Variables shared between several components: The monitor parts of all
components are merged into a single monitor to ensure mutual exclusion
between the transitions of different components.

(b) A component X is hierarchically dependent on a component Y (i.e. transitions of X are only possible when Y is in a particular state; see [5]):
The monitor part of X is realized as a class declared as local variable
or parameter inside the monitor part of Y. The process part of X accesses
this class via the monitor part of Y.

(c) Two components X and Y are directly coupled (i.e. certain transitions
of X may only be executed in parallel with certain transitions of Y;
see [5]): The monitor part of one component is realized as a class
declared inside the monitor part of the other component, similarly to
the case above.

As an example, figure 7 shows the inner structure of the packet sender module.
In addition to the *Primary link set-up* component, already shown in figure 6,
this figure also shows the realization of the other components of the module,
(see figure 2), and the *Link manager* monitor (see section 4 below). To
explain the relations shown in the figure, we note that a sending transition,
for instance, is activated by the *Frame sender* process calling an operation of
the *Primary link set-up* monitor. The latter performs a link set-up, reset or
disconnection transition, if appropriate (depending on its own state and the
Link manager), and otherwise calls an operation of the *Source* class which, in
turn, may perform a sending transition. Any transition performed is coordinated
with the *PF control* class which sets the poll/final bit of the frame to be sent.
Appendix A shows the detailed coding of the *Primary link set-up* monitor in
Concurrent Pascal.

The transformation rules for obtaining a protocol implementation
from its formalized specification should be straightforward in order to avoid
programming errors. This is the case for the rules discussed so far. However,
we found that the following two aspects of the transformation involved more
complex decisions, and are therefore more subject to errors:

(1) The non-determinism inherent in the transition diagram must be eliminated,
which implies an ordering of the transitions and some rearrangement of the
enabling predicates in order to obtain efficient test sequences. The
transition actions may also be rearranged in order to eliminate redundancy.

(2) To avoid busy waiting in the case when no transition is enabled, a calling
process must *wait* in the monitor until another process changes the component
state. This change must be *signalled* to the waiting process. It is not
always easy to decide when, and to which process, a signal must be sent (for
an example, see appendix A).

An example of non-determinism is given by the transitions <u>SARM</u> and
<u>DISC</u> possible in the *connected* state of the *Primary link set-up* component (see
figure 3(a)). While the choice between these two transitions is left completely
open by the formalized specification of [5] (see figure 3(d)), the choice is
largely determined by the enabling predicates in our formalized specification
(see figure 3(c)). However, a system state is possible for which both transitions are enabled. In our implementation (see the appendix), we have given a
priority to the <u>DISC</u> transition.

4. THE STRUCTURE OF THE X.25 IMPLEMENTATION

The general structure of the X.25 implementation is shown in figure 8.
The physical layer of X.25 is implemented in the line controller hardware, and
not shown.

The structure of the link layer is obtained by applying the transformations discussed above to the structure of figure 1. The three *Frame sender*
and *receiver* processes activate the transitions of the primary and secondary
link components. The piggy-backing of acknowledgments is performed in the
Output frame buffer, which also performs the multiplexing of frames from the
primary and secondary link components over the output circuit. The demultiplexing of incoming frames on to the primary and secondary link components is
performed by the *Frame receiver* process. This process activates the receiving
transitions of both components. Two separate *receiver* processes could have been
used to allow for full parallelism between the sending and receiving of packets.
The *Input* and *Output* processes activate the frame input and output, and perform
the transmission error detection, frame delimitation and transparency functions.
In our implementation, these functions are mainly realized in software by the
Concurrent Pascal system kernel [7] via IO commands executed by the *Input*
and *Output* processes. Clearly, these functions would be more efficiently
implemented by a separate hardware processor.

The operation of the link layer is supervised by a *Link manager*. It
determines whether the link to the network should be established, disconnected
or reset, and coordinates the operation of the primary and secondary components.
The latter, in turn, report to the link manager those errors which cannot be
recovered by the link level procedures. The interface between the *Link manager*
and the *Primary link* component, for instance, is described in figure 3(b), and
its use is shown in appendix A.

The interface between the link and packet layers is very simple.
It consists of two primitives for sending and receiving a packet, respectively.
We note that the calling processes may be delayed due to flow control conside-
rations (see section 5.2 below).

The transformation principles, described above, were also applied to
the VC *control* module of the packet level. As in the case of the link layer,
a single process, the *Packet receiver* (see figure 8), performs the demultiplexing of incoming packets into the different VC's, and activates the receiving
transitions of all *VC control* monitors. For the multiplexing of outgoing
packets, an approach different from the link layer was adopted. Instead of
having independent packet sending processes, one for each VC, a single *Packet
sender* process looks after all VC's and receives requests for packet transmission through a *Scheduling* monitor. This monitor is the place where different
priorities may be introduced for the different VC's. The control of each VC

is partitioned into a module responible for observing the X.25 packet level
procedures, and a module which provides a VC interface to the next higher
layers of the computer system. In particular, the latter module provides
flow control functions, automatic answering of clear, reset and interrupt
indication packets, and a time-out function for call, clear, and reset
requests and interrupts [8] .

We have tried to design a reasonable VC interface to the higher
layers following the X.25 specifications as closely as possible. The resulting
interface may be characterized by the following primitives:

- restart-request
- call-request (...)
- wait-for-incoming-call (...)
- accept-call
- clear-request
- reset-request
- send-interrupt (...)
- send-data (...)
- receive-data (...)
- get-new-status.

Each of these primitives, called by the higher layer, returns VC status
information, which includes

(a) information about the present state of the interface, such as

- restarted by DTE or DCE,
- connected by DTE or DCE,
- disconnected by DTE or DCE,
- reset by DTE or DCE,
- interrupt sent by DTE or received from DCE,
- time out, i.e. the primitive returned control to the higher level before
  the system received an appropriate packet form the network (DCE) in
  response to a request from the system

(b) flow control, i.e. indication that received data is available, or no
buffer space is available for sending more data

(c) error indications, such as

- procedure errors of the network
- invalidity of a request from the higher layer in the present interface
  state.

5. STEPWISE REFINEMENT AND IMPLEMENTATION CHOICES

5.1. General remarks

Our X.25 implementation effort may be considered as an exercise in step-wise refinement. The first step is the establishment of the formalized protocol specification described in section 2. Further steps, some of which are described in sections 3 and 4, lead towards the implemented system which is described in full in [2] . In sections 3 and 4, we have described the choices that lead from the system structure of figure 1, which consists of message driven modules the operation of which are described by the formalized protocol specification, to the structure of figure 8, which is based on the monitor, class and process primitives available in the implementation language.

However, there are many more implementation choices to be made. They mainly concern the implementation of classes and monitors for which, so far, only the interfaces have been defined. Examples are the *Link manager* component, which in our system is implemented as a monitor and process interacting with the operator, and the buffer management described below. For both modules, the interface has been used in the formalized protocol specification. A complete list of all program components is given in appendix B.

Our effort for obtaining the X.25 implementation may be subdivided into the following steps, each of which took about one man month of work:

- to derive the formalized specification of the link and packet level procedures (given the specification in [5])
- to design the structure of the system, such as shown in the figures 7, 8 and 9, and in appendix B (this includes the development of the implementation transformations described in section 3),
- to write the program components in Concurrent Pascal, and
- to test and and debug the system.

5.2. Buffer management and flow control

Buffer queues for the intermediate storage of packets or frames, between any pair of cooperating processes, have been foreseen in the system as indicated in figure 8. These queues control the information flow within the system, and synchronize the relative speeds of the different processes in the system, since a process accessing a queue has to wait until it is not empty, or not full respectively. The only exception is the *Input* process which is not delayed when the *Input frame buffer* is full. Instead, the last frame is lost.

In order to avoid unnecessary copying of data packets from one queue to another during the processing of the packets within the system, the frames coming in from the network, as well as the data packets from the higher system layers are stored within a centrally managed buffer space and subsequently referred to by pointers. Therefore, the information exchanged between the system components shown in figure 8, includes these pointers, together with other control information, but not the copies of data packets.

In order to simplify the avoidance of deadlocks, a fixed number of packets, or frames respectively, is allocated as the maximum length for each of the queues. The total space required may be determined according to the equation

$$\left.\begin{array}{l}\text{total number} \\ \text{of blocks}\end{array}\right\} = \sum_i \text{maximum number of blocks in queue } i$$

$$+ \sum_j \begin{array}{l}\text{number of blocks not in a queue and being} \\ \text{processed by process } j.\end{array}$$

The structure of the buffer management facility is shown in figure 9, which shows the central buffer manager (a monitor) and the different buffer queues (classes). The queue of the *Primary link* is completed by a class providing additional management facilities needed for packet retransmission. The central buffer manager may also be directly accessed, to obtain a new block, change or read the information stored in a block, or free a block.

5.3.   *Message coding*

For compatibility with the remote communication partner, a protocol specifies the exact layout of information fields within the exchanged messages. This message format must be implemented by the communications software, and involves the specification of memory layout of structured data, bit packing, etc. It is not possible to describe these details in a single software module, since each protocol layer, separately, specifies the layout of the corresponding message header. An implementation language with facilities for specifying memory layout of packed data structures would be convenient for this purpose.

Our implementation language did not provide this facility, therefore the coding and decoding of the packet and frame headers is implemented in several different procedures. The central buffer manager provides operations for reading and writing selected octets of a given data block. These operations may also be used by higher level protocols. Specific procedures are included in the *Packet sender* and *receiver* processes (for packet header (de-)coding), and in the *Frame receiver* and *Output frame buffer* (for HDLC header (de-)coding).

6.   *CONCLUDING REMARKS*

6.1.   *The use of a formalized protocol specification*

As explained in sections 2 and 3, we have developed a formalized specification of X.25 which served as the basis for the implementation. We would have appreciated a more formalized specification of the X.25 standard which could have saved us this effort. A formalized protocol specification not only has the advantage of simplifying the implementation, but is also useful during the protocol design, verification and evaluation phase (see for example [9]).

6.2.   The use of a high-level implementation language

We conclude form our experience that the following properties of the implementation language were most valuable for the project:

(a) Facilities for step-wise refinement, in particular the *class* concept.

(b) Facilities for describing parallel activities. We used the *processes* and *monitors* of Concurrent Pascal, however, we would have appreciated a language construct (see for example [2]) closely related to the *component* structure described in section 2.1.

(c) The facilities for type definition and checking, common to most Pascal-like languages.

Other aspects of our language implementation were not entirely satisfactory, such as for example its low efficiency and the inability to interwork with the standard computer operating system.

An advantage of using a high-level implementation language is the reduction of the programming and testing effort required. The testing of each protocol layer was done in two phases. First the system was embedded, on the same computer, in a testing environment, also written in Concurrent Pascal. Secondly, the system was checked with an X.25 protocol tester equipment which was connected to the computer via the data network access line. Both phases were effective.

We believe that a high-level language implementation such as ours, is useful even when the high-level programming language is not implemented on the target computer, or when the efficiency or operating system interfaces of the implementation are insufficient. Efficiency may be increased by reprogramming the critical procedures in machine language; or the whole program may be used as a "blueprint" for an implementation in a suitable language. We note that Belsnes [10] comes to similar conclusions, describing an implementation of X.25 in Simula.

6.3.   The VC interface

In section 4, we described, in some detail, the VC interface, which is the interface between the X.25 network access module and the remaining part of the computer system. In deriving this interface from the X.25 packet level specifications, we were astonished by the great complexity of the resulting interface. We wonder whether an interface to an end-to-end transport service [11] would be simpler in nature. A criterion for the delimitation of major system modules is the simplicity of the resulting interfaces. The experience with our X.25 implementation has not convinced us that the X.25 VC is a natural system interface.

6.4.   Implementation on multiple microprocessors

In a microprocessor based implementation of X.25, the different protocol layers may be distributed over several microprocessors [12,13] . To avoid memory bus congestion, each microprocessor usually has its own local memory, which contains the program code and processed data, and may exchange messages, via a system bus, with the other microprocessors in the system. A system described in terms of processes and monitors, such as shown in figure 8, is suitable for distribution over a multi-microprocessor system. A possible distribution method, called "split process organization" by Cavers [12] , proceeds as follows. First each monitor of the system is allocated to a suitable microprocessor. Then the processes are allocated. Processes accessing the monitors in one microprocessor are allocated to that microprocessor. Processes accessing monitors in more than one microprocessor are split into subprocesses, one for each microprocessor involved and allocated to it. The subprocesses communicate by message exchange via the system bus. This organization is particularly appropriate when most processing in the system is done in the monitors, and the processes have essentially the role of passing information. This is the case in the X.25 system of figure 8.

ACKNOWLEDGEMENTS

We thank Pierre Desjardins for many useful discussions, and the Concurrent Pascal implementation on the Xerox Sigma-6 computer used for our implementation. We are grateful to the Computer Communications Group of Bell Canada for letting us use their X.25 tester equipment. Finally, we thank Simon Waddel for a revision of the manuscript, and Mme Luyet for the careful typing.

REFERENCES

1.   CCITT Recommendation X.25 (1976).

2.   Tankoano Joachim, "Implantation du protocole standard X.25 à partir d'un modèle de formalisation et de mécanismes abstraits de programmation", Master's thesis, Département d'IRO, Université de Montréal, Dec. 1977.

3.   P. Brinch-Hansen, "The programming language Concurrent Pascal", IEEE Trans. on Software Eng., SE-1 (1975), pp. 199-207.

4.   G.V. Bochmann and J. Gecsei, "A unified model for the specification and verification of protocols", Proc. IFIP Congress 1977, North Holland, Amsterdam, pp. 229-234.

5.   G.V. Bochmann et R.J. Chung, "A formalized description of HDLC classes of procedures", Proc. Nat. Telecomm. Conf., IEEE, 1977, pp. 03A. .2-1 to 2-11.

6.   H.A. Schmid, "On the efficient implementation of conditional critical regions and the construction of monitors", Acta Informatica 6 (1976), pp. 227-249.

7.   P. Desjardins, "Un pilote pour controleur de communication dans Solo-Sigma", Technical report (in preparation), Département d'I.R.O., Université de Montréal.

8.   A.M. Rybczynski, Collection of questions and answers on X.25, Working document, 1977.

9.   G.V. Bochmann, "Specification and verification of computer communication protocols", Publication #294, Département d'I.R.O., Université de Montréal, 1978.

10.   D. Belsnes , "X.25 DTE implement in Simula", Proc. Eurocomp 78, 1978, Online, England.

11. IFIP Working Group 6.1, "Proposal for an internetwork end-to-end transport protocol", INWG Note 96.X, also in Proc. Computer Network Protocols Symposium, Université de Liège, 1978.

12. J.K. Cavers, "Implementation of X.25 on a multiple micro-processor system", Proc. Intern. Comm. Conference, 1978.

13. D.L.A. Barber, T. Kalin and C. Solomonides, "An implementation of the X.25 interface in a datagram network", Proc. Computer Network Protocols Symposium, Université de Liège, 1978, pp. /6-1 to E6-5.

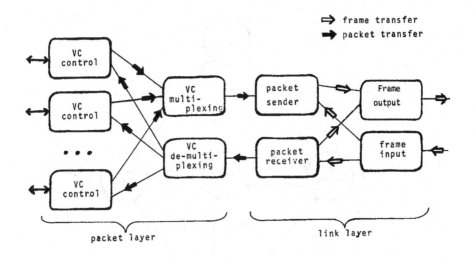

FIGURE 1

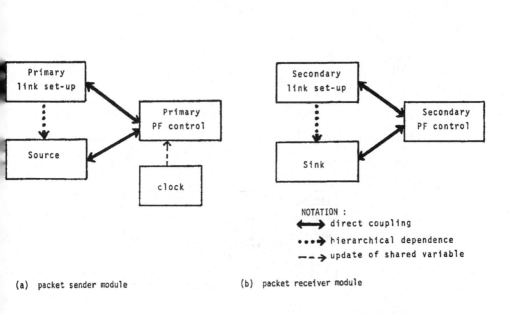

(a) packet sender module

(b) packet receiver module

FIGURE 2

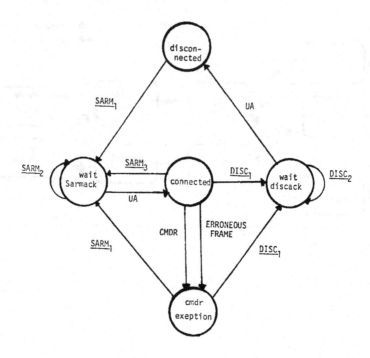

Fig. 3 (a)

```
┌────────────────────────────────────────────┐
│ variables                                  │
│                                            │
│ ERRCOUNT:  integer;                        │
│                                            │
│ HIGHLEVEL:  interface of Link manager;     │
│    CONNECT:  booléan;                       │
│    DISCONNECT:  booléan;                    │
│    REPORTCMDR;                              │
│    ERROR;                                   │
└────────────────────────────────────────────┘
```

FIGURE 3(b)

Transition	Prédicat d'activation	Action	Signification
$\underline{SARM_1}$	HIGHLEVEL.CONNECT	ERRCOUNT:=0 PFCONTROLPRIMARY.BIT:=1 INIT (TRANSMIT,SARM); *Send* (TRANSMIT);	invite le DCE à se mettre en mode de communication asynchrone
$\underline{SARM_3}$	LINKSOURCE.ERRCOUNT=MAXERRCOUNT	- idem -	- idem - (cas de retransmission)
$\underline{SARM_2}$	LINKCLOCK.TIMEOUT ∧ ERRCOUNT < MAXERRCOUNT	ERRCOUNT:=ERRCOUNT + 1; PFCONTROLPRIMARY.BIT:=1; INIT(TRANSMIT,SARM); *Send*(TRANSMIT);	- idem -
$\underline{DISC_1}$	HIGHLEVEL.DISCONNECT	ERRCOUNT:=0 PFCONTROLPRIMARY.BIT:=1 INIT(TRANSMIT,DISC); *Send*(TRANSMIT);	invite le DCE à se déconnecter
$\underline{DISC_2}$	LINKCLOCK.TIMEOUT ∧ ERRCOUNT < MAXERRCOUNT	ERRCOUNT:=ERRCOUNT + 1; PFCONTROLPRIMARY.BIT:=1; INIT(TRANSMIT,DISC); *Send*(TRANSMIT);	- idem - (cas de retransmission)
UA	RECEIVED.KIND=UA ∧ RECEIVED.FBIT = 1	LINKSOURCE.*initialisation*;	Met la composante LINKSOURCE dans son état initial
CMDR	RECEIVED.KIND = CMDR	HIGHLEVEL.REPORTCMDR;	informe le niveau supérieur qu'une trame a été rejetée
ERRONEOUSFRAME	RECEIVED.KIND =ERRONEOUSFRAME	HIGHLEVEL.ERROR;	informe le niveau supérieur qu'une trame erronée a été reçue

Fig. 3(c)

2.3.4.5 *Set Asynchronous Response Mode (SARM) Command*
The SARM unnumbered command is used to place the addressed secondary in the Asynchronous Response Mode (ARM).

No information field is permitted with the SARM command. A secondary confirms acceptance of SARM by the transmission at the first opportunity of a UA response Upon acceptance of this command, the secondary receive state variable is set to zero.

Previously transmitted frames that are unacknowledged when this command is actioned remain unacknowledged.

2 4.3.1 *Link Setup*
The DCE will indicate that it is able to set up the link by transmitting contiguous flags (active channel state).

The DTE shall indicate a request for setting up the link by transmitting a SARM command to the DCE.

Whenever receiving a SARM command, the DCE will return a UA response to the DTE and set its receive state variable V(R) to zero.

Should the DCE wish to indicate a request for setting up the link, or when receiving from the DTE a first SARM command as a request for setting up the link, the DCE will transmit a SARM command to the DTE and start timer T1 (see Section 2 4.7). The DTE will confirm the reception of the SARM command by transmitting a UA response.

When receiving the UA response, the DCE will set its send state variable V(S) to zero and stop its timer T1. If timer T1 runs out before the UA response is received by the DCE, the DCE will retransmit a SARM command and restart timer T1

After transmission of SARM N2 times by the DCE, appropriate recovery action will be initiated
The value of N2 is defined in Section 2 4.7

2.3.5.6 *Rejection Condition*
A rejection condition is established upon the receipt of an error-free frame which contains an invalid command/response in the control field, an invalid frame format, an invalid N(R) count, or an information field which exceeded the maximum information field length which can be accommodated

At the primary this exception is subject to recovery/resolution at a higher function level

2.4.5.5 If the DCE transmits a CMDR response, it enters the command rejection condition This command rejection condition is cleared when the DCE receives a SARM or DISC command. Any other command received while in the command rejection condition will cause the DCE to retransmit this CMDR response The coding of the CMDR response will be as described in Section 2.3.4.8. In the case of an invalid N(S), bits 4, 5, 6, and 7 of octet 3 will be set to zero

Fig. 3(e)

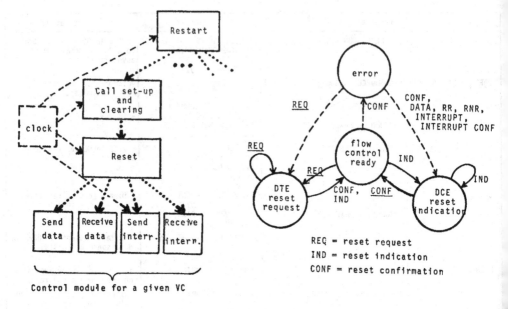

Control module for a given VC

REQ = reset request
IND = reset indication
CONF = reset confirmation

FIGURE 4   FIGURE 5

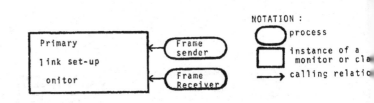

NOTATION :

⬭ process

▭ instance of a
   monitor or cla

→ calling relatio

FIGURE 6

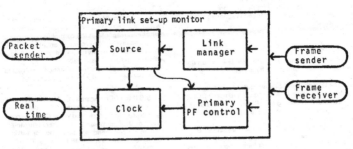

FIGURE 7

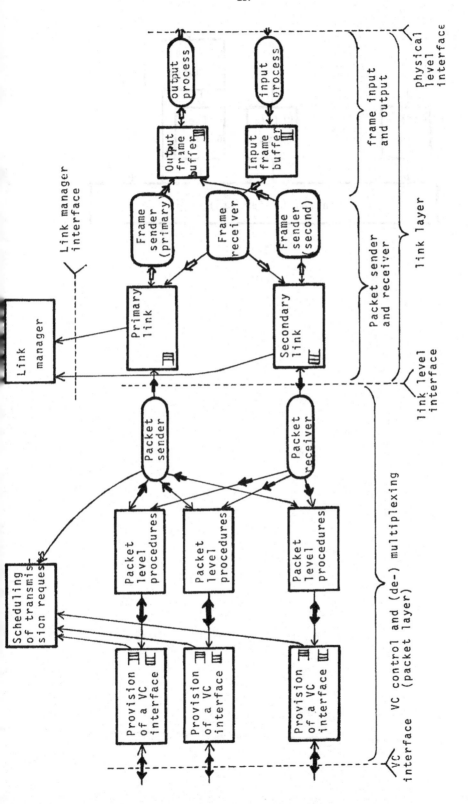

FIGURE 8

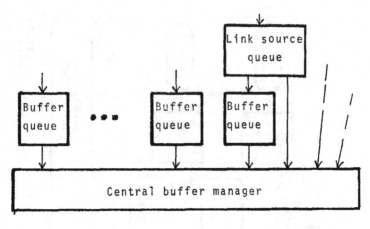

FIGURE   9

Vol. 49: Interactive Systems. Proceedings 1976. Edited by A. Blaser and C. Hackl. VI, 380 pages. 1976.

Vol. 50: A. C. Hartmann, A Concurrent Pascal Compiler for Mini-computers. VI, 119 pages. 1977.

Vol. 51: B. S. Garbow, Matrix Eigensystem Routines – Eispack Guide Extension. VIII, 343 pages. 1977.

Vol. 52: Automata, Languages and Programming. Fourth Colloquium, University of Turku, July 1977. Edited by A. Salomaa and M. Steinby. X, 569 pages. 1977.

Vol. 53: Mathematical Foundations of Computer Science. Proceedings 1977. Edited by J. Gruska. XII, 608 pages. 1977.

Vol. 54: Design and Implementation of Programming Languages. Proceedings 1976. Edited by J. H. Williams and D. A. Fisher. X, 496 pages. 1977.

Vol. 55: A. Gerbier, Mes premières constructions de programmes. XII, 256 pages. 1977.

Vol. 56: Fundamentals of Computation Theory. Proceedings 1977. Edited by M. Karpiński. XII, 542 pages. 1977.

Vol. 57: Portability of Numerical Software. Proceedings 1976. Edited by W. Cowell. VIII, 539 pages. 1977.

Vol. 58: M. J. O'Donnell, Computing in Systems Described by Equations. XIV, 111 pages. 1977.

Vol. 59: E. Hill, Jr., A Comparative Study of Very Large Data Bases. X, 140 pages. 1978.

Vol. 60: Operating Systems, An Advanced Course. Edited by R. Bayer, R. M. Graham, and G. Seegmüller. X, 593 pages. 1978.

Vol. 61: The Vienna Development Method: The Meta-Language. Edited by D. Bjørner and C. B. Jones. XVIII, 382 pages. 1978.

Vol. 62: Automata, Languages and Programming. Proceedings 1978. Edited by G. Ausiello and C. Böhm. VIII, 508 pages. 1978.

Vol. 63: Natural Language Communication with Computers. Edited by Leonard Bolc. VI, 292 pages. 1978.

Vol. 64: Mathematical Foundations of Computer Science. Proceedings 1978. Edited by J. Winkowski. X, 551 pages. 1978.

Vol. 65: Information Systems Methodology, Proceedings, 1978. Edited by G. Bracchi and P. C. Lockemann. XII, 696 pages. 1978.

Vol. 66: N. D. Jones and S. S. Muchnick, TEMPO: A Unified Treatment of Binding Time and Parameter Passing Concepts in Programming Languages. IX, 118 pages. 1978.

Vol. 67: Theoretical Computer Science, 4th GI Conference, Aachen, March 1979. Edited by K. Weihrauch. VII, 324 pages. 1979.

Vol. 68: D. Harel, First-Order Dynamic Logic. X, 133 pages. 1979.

Vol. 69: Program Construction. International Summer School. Edited by F. L. Bauer and M. Broy. VII, 651 pages. 1979.

Vol. 70: Semantics of Concurrent Computation. Proceedings 1979. Edited by G. Kahn. VI, 368 pages. 1979.

Vol. 71: Automata, Languages and Programming. Proceedings 1979. Edited by H. A. Maurer. IX, 684 pages. 1979.

Vol. 72: Symbolic and Algebraic Computation. Proceedings 1979. Edited by E. W. Ng. XV, 557 pages. 1979.

Vol. 73: Graph-Grammars and Their Application to Computer Science and Biology. Proceedings 1978. Edited by V. Claus, H. Ehrig and G. Rozenberg. VII, 477 pages. 1979.

Vol. 74: Mathematical Foundations of Computer Science. Proceedings 1979. Edited by J. Bečvář. IX, 580 pages. 1979.

Vol. 75: Mathematical Studies of Information Processing. Proceedings 1978. Edited by E. K. Blum, M. Paul and S. Takasu. VIII, 629 pages. 1979.

Vol. 76: Codes for Boundary-Value Problems in Ordinary Differential Equations. Proceedings 1978. Edited by B. Childs et al. VIII, 388 pages. 1979.

Vol. 77: G. V. Bochmann, Architecture of Distributed Computer Systems. VIII, 238 pages. 1979.